EXPLORING
HAVASUPAI

A GUIDE TO THE HEART
OF THE GRAND CANYON

2ND EDITION

GREG WITT

MENASHA RIDGE PRESS
BIRMINGHAM, ALABAMA

EXPLORING HAVASUPAI

A Guide to the Heart of the Grand Canyon

Copyright © 2017 by Greg Witt
All rights reserved
Published by Menasha Ridge Press
Manufactured in China
Distributed by Publishers Group West
Second edition, third printing 2020

Cover and text design: Lora Westberg
Cartography: Scott McGrew and Greg Witt
Cover photographs: *front,* Shutterstock; *back,* iStock©fremme
Interior photographs: Greg Witt, David Crowther, Amy Sorensen, and stock unless otherwise noted
Author photograph: Harriet Friedman

Library of Congress Cataloging-in-Publication Data
Names: Witt, Greg, 1952- author.
Title: Exploring Havasupai : a guide to the heart of the Grand Canyon / Greg Witt.
Description: Second edition. | Birmingham, Alabama : Menasha Ridge Press,
   [2016] | Series: Five-Star Trails | "Distributed by Publishers Group
   West"—T.p. verso. | Includes index.
Identifiers: LCCN 2016039680| ISBN 9781634040709 (paperback) |
   ISBN 9781634040716 (ebook); ISBN 9781634042116 (hardcover)
Subjects: LCSH: Havasupai Reservation (Ariz.)—Guidebooks. | Havasupai
   Indians—Social life and customs. | Natural history—Arizona—Havasupai
   Reservation—Guidebooks. | Trails—Arizona—Havasupai
   Reservation—Guidebooks. | Hiking—Arizona—Havasupai
   Reservation—Guidebooks. | Grand Canyon (Ariz.)—Guidebooks.
Classification: LCC E99.H3 W58 2016 | DDC 979.1/32—dc23
LC record available at https://lccn.loc.gov/2016039680

Menasha Ridge Press
An imprint of AdventureKEEN
2204 First Ave. S., Suite 102
Birmingham, AL 35233
800-443-7227, fax 205-326-1012

Visit menasharidge.com for a complete listing of our books and for ordering information. Contact
us at our website, at facebook.com/menasharidge, or at twitter.com/menasharidge with questions or
comments. To find out more about who we are and what we're doing, visit blog.menasharidge.com.

TABLE OF CONTENTS

ABOUT THE AUTHOR

Author Greg Witt at Mooney Falls

Greg Witt's journeys have taken him to every corner of the globe. He has guided mountaineering expeditions in the Alps and Andes and paddled wild rivers in the Americas. He has dropped teams of adventurers into golden slot canyons; trudged through deep jungles in Africa, Central America, and Asia; and guided archaeological expeditions across the parched Arabian Peninsula. His passion for adventure has always focused on sharing his experience with others.

Following degrees from the University of California and Brigham Young University, he had an early career in human resources management; but Greg prefers high adventure to the high-rise, so decades ago he traded his wingtips for hiking boots and has never looked back.

Some weeks, Greg hikes more miles than he drives, which means he wears out his boots faster than he wears out his tires. He has crossed the Grand Canyon on foot more than a dozen times, climbed Colorado's three highest peaks in three days, and each summer as a guide in the Alps he hikes more than 700 miles and gains nearly 100,000 vertical feet of elevation—the equivalent of climbing Everest 9 times.

Now he leads readers on the most breathtaking hikes and exciting outdoor adventures on the globe. He comes ready to discuss the geology, history, archaeology, weather patterns, culture, and flora and fauna of the exciting locales he loves. His other titles include *60 Hikes Within 60 Miles: Salt Lake City* and *50 Best Short Hikes in Utah's National Parks*. Greg's research and exploration continue to uncover the unknown. If you join him, you can be guaranteed a phenomenal adventure peppered with the unexpected.

ACKNOWLEDGMENTS

Havasupai's natural splendor has been preserved to enjoy today due to the gentle stewardship of the Havasupai tribe, who call this canyon their home. They have been both gracious and cautious in sharing their tribal home with visitors from around the world. Their assistance with this book has been invaluable.

The people of Menasha Ridge Press have been especially trusting as they decided to publish a book on a rather obscure and remote destination, knowing it would enhance the experience for every visitor wanting to see Havasupai's plunging waterfalls and steep canyon walls. Thanks to Molly Merkle, Steve Jones, Travis Bryant, Scott McGrew, and Holly Cross.

My hiking companion and dear friend Alan Colledge, whose love for the people and canyon spans more than three decades, first enticed me to visit Havasupai. On our first hike into the canyon he suggested that visitors need a detailed and thorough guidebook to the area. It has taken years. Here it is.

Special thanks to the Havasupai Tribal Council and particularly to the efforts of Chairman Don Watahomigie and Vice Chairman Matthew Putesoy, who oversaw much of the recovery following the August 2008 flood. Many thanks to Lawrence Carson, Rex Tilousi, and Roland Manakaja, who provided insights into the tribe's history and shared their devotion to the canyon and its people.

Professional photographer Derek von Briesen was especially gracious with his time and professional talents in assisting with this book. Photographs by David Crowther and Amy Sorensen also add a colorful accent.

And thanks to my wife, Elain, who is willing to risk sunburn, blisters, and bruises to join me on my wilderness adventures. She has been an unwavering source of encouragement, love, and support on this project. Exploring Havasupai or anywhere with her is always a joy.

CHAPTER 1
HAVASUPAI: THE HEART OF THE GRAND CANYON

Paradise has never been easily reached. In the case of Havasupai, it's 10 miles on foot or by horse from a canyon-rim trailhead that's still 60 miles removed from the old Route 66 in northern Arizona. By most standards, Supai Village, which lies in the depths of Havasu Canyon, is the most remote town in the continental United States and the only community remaining where both the mail and the trash are still carried out by mules.

In this canyon paradise, color, form, and light create a scenic palette with a distinctive and unmatched appeal. Red canyon walls, deep-green cottonwoods, a cloudless desert sky, and pearlescent limestone combine to reflect a turquoise hue from the waters of Havasu Creek. Iridescent shades of aquamarine bounce off glistening pools, and thunderous waterfalls throw sprays that form rainbows.

Every day Havasu Creek carries 38 million gallons of natural spring water into the Grand Canyon of the Colorado River. Along the way it nourishes the Supai Village—its farms, livestock, and people. As the creek slithers down the canyon, abrupt cliffs form some of the most spectacular waterfalls imaginable, while travertine rims create hundreds of natural pools and drops. The perennial flow of Havasu Creek sustains more life—both people and agricultural production—than any other tributary within the Grand Canyon. Providing the necessary water for the tribe and its livelihood, this spring-fed stream is also the primary attraction for the thousands of visitors who come to the canyon each year.

Most visitors to the Grand Canyon drive from one crowded overlook to the next and never experience the inner beauty of the canyon. For those willing to pay the price of strapping on a pair of boots or saddling up, Havasupai reveals its variety of natural wonders. Tucked away like a sun-drenched Shangri-la, this stunning red-rock oasis must be deliberately and thoughtfully sought out. There are steep and jagged miles between the trailhead and your first glimpse of water. Blistering sun, choking dust, and steep canyon walls accompany you on your journey. With each footfall, you dream of pristine aquamarine pools and tumbling waterfalls. The vision keeps you plodding onward until the blasting desert inferno is suddenly subdued by cooling mist, draping ferns, and leafy cottonwoods—you have arrived at Havasupai.

Once in the canyon, you can indulge your senses in a thousand ways. You can cool yourself in the crystalline waters of the creek or soak in bubbling pools. You can nap in dappled shade to the roar of a thunderous lullaby or explore hidden grottos and uncharted channels of the creek. Side canyons can be sun-baked, dry, and rocky or dark, moist, and blanketed with dripping ferns. By nightfall, the desert air cools and even brings a welcome chill in the spring and fall.

The native people of Havasu Canyon, those who call themselves *Havasuw 'Baaja*—people of the blue-green water—comprise a tribe of about 650 members known as the Havasupai. Most of the tribe members live in the Supai Village, where they speak their native Havasupai language and farm on tribal lands. They are the only indigenous people of the Grand Canyon living in the canyon today. A resourceful people, they are keepers of an ancient heritage and rightfully proud of their home.

As people from around the world learn about Havasupai and the incomparable beauty of the canyon, they find their way to the trailhead, to the village, and on to the falls and pools. Today tourism forms the economic base for the tribe and provides jobs in packing supplies on horseback and in operating the lodge, campground, café, and store. Other tribal members are employed in tribal-run federal programs and in municipal services. But sharing the natural wonders of Havasupai with the world comes at a high price. Trail maintenance, construction of facilities, and waste management are all expensive and difficult undertakings in this remote landscape.

Edward Abbey's Visit to Havasupai

Edward Abbey, the ever-eloquent anarchist of the American Southwest, offered this account of his visit to Havasupai:

One summer I started off to visit for the first time the city of Los Angeles. I was riding with some friends from the University of New Mexico. On the way we stopped off briefly to roll an old tire into the Grand Canyon. While watching the tire bounce over tall pine trees, tear hell out of a mule train and disappear with a final grand leap into the inner gorge, I overheard the park ranger standing nearby say a few words about a place called Havasu, or Havasupai. A branch, it seemed, of the Grand Canyon.

What I heard made me think that I should see Havasu immediately, before something went wrong somewhere. My friends said they would wait. So I went down into Havasu—fourteen miles by trail—and looked things over. When I returned five weeks later I discovered that the others had gone on to Los Angeles without me.

That was fifteen years ago. And still I have not seen the fabulous city on the Pacific shore. Perhaps I never will. . . .

But Havasu. Once down in there it's hard to get out. . . . I bought a slab of bacon and six cans of beans at the village post office, rented a large comfortable horse, and proceeded farther down the canyon . . . to the ruins of an old mining camp five miles below the village. There I lived, mostly alone except for the ghosts, for the next thirty-five days.

There was nothing wrong with the Indians. The Supai are a charming cheerful completely relaxed and easygoing bunch, all one hundred or so of them. But I had no desire to live among them unless clearly invited to do so, and I wasn't. Even if invited I might not have accepted. I'm not sure that I care for the idea of strangers examining my daily habits and folk-ways, studying my language, inspecting my costume, questioning me about my religion, classifying my artifacts, investigating my sexual rites, and evaluating my chances for cultural survival.

So I lived alone.

From Desert Solitaire © 1968 by Edward Abbey

EXPLORING HAVASUPAI is packed with the essential information you need to make your trip to Havasupai spectacular. You will come to understand and appreciate the history of the native people of the canyon, the Havasupai. Specific information is given on what you will need to bring for your safety and comfort in this remote corner of the Grand Canyon. The guide is loaded with detailed instructions on how to find and enjoy every rich element of this piece of paradise—from hidden waterfalls to limestone caverns to dramatic overlooks. Sprinkled throughout are fascinating and informative morsels of history, geology, folklore, weather, and nature that will make your visit even more meaningful. And woven into each page of this guide is a reverence for the land and people that will help you sense your responsibility to leave the canyon every bit as perfect as you found it.

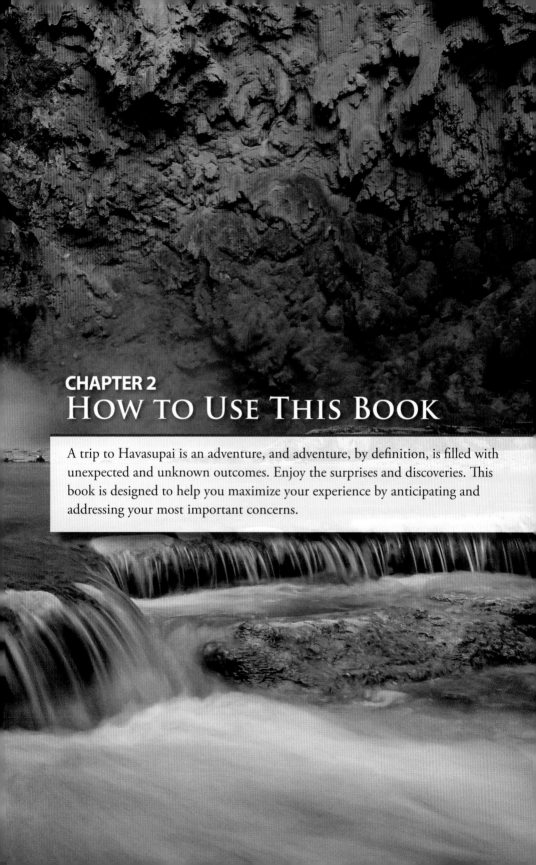

CHAPTER 2
HOW TO USE THIS BOOK

A trip to Havasupai is an adventure, and adventure, by definition, is filled with unexpected and unknown outcomes. Enjoy the surprises and discoveries. This book is designed to help you maximize your experience by anticipating and addressing your most important concerns.

DISTANCES

All of the distances in this book are derived from odometer and GPS readings and are accurate to the nearest tenth of a mile. On some of the lesser-known trails, previous publications have relied on estimates. The measurements given here reflect the first time these hikes have been measured, recorded, and published.

TIMES

Hiking times have been tested under varying conditions and take into account the added time required for crossing creeks, climbing steep slopes, or scrambling up boulder-strewn canyon draws. The minimum time shown assumes someone in good physical condition, walking in mild weather, and taking minimal breaks. Expect longer times in hot weather, where a less-strenuous pace and more frequent water breaks are recommended.

RATINGS

Difficulty ratings for trails are general guidelines. One hiker's moderate trail may be another hiker's extremely strenuous trail. But generally you'll find these ratings correspond with those given for similar trails in national parks and other popular hiking destinations.

The ratings for hikes take into consideration the distance, elevation gain, lack of shade, navigational challenges, and any difficult scrambling or climbing. The rating also considers that for some trails you will have already hiked several miles to access the trailhead. The Beaver Canyon hike, for example, is accessible only to those who have already hiked down to Beaver Falls.

Coconino Cliffs

DIRECTIONS

All desert canyons are full of winding surprises. The Colorado River, which generally flows from east to west through the Grand Canyon, can, at any given point, flow from north to south, south to north, or even southwest to northeast.

For the purpose of this guidebook, Havasu Canyon and Havasu Creek are described as running from south to north. All side canyons are described as running from east to west or west to east, even though a precise compass reading may give you a somewhat different orientation. The benefits of this simplified approach will become evident as you explore the canyons of Havasupai.

GPS COORDINATES

Within the narrow side canyons of Havasupai, a GPS device has its limitations. Tracking a satellite signal is rarely a problem in the wider sections of Hualapai Canyon. But as the canyon narrows, and particularly in some of the deep side canyon hikes described in this guide, locating a satellite may be impossible. Fortunately, in Havasupai most navigation is guided by the course of the creek and walls of the canyon, so getting lost is rarely a concern.

You may find that the maps in this book provide ample assistance for most navigational needs and that the GPS coordinates are superfluous. You're probably right; in which case you can just think of the GPS locators as free bonus material. However, there are some surprises and decoys on many of these trails. More than one hiker has turned around at Upper Beaver Falls (or False Beaver, as it's known), missing the real deal just a few minutes downstream. If the GPS coordinates can save you that kind of mistake or eliminate the need to do 30 minutes of backtracking on some mesa trail, their inclusion is worth it.

TIPS FROM A PROFESSIONAL PHOTOGRAPHER

Photo tips are from Derek von Briesen, a Sedona-based professional landscape photographer specializing in capturing the outdoor beauty of Arizona and the American Southwest. His images have appeared in *National Geographic,* and he regularly conducts photography workshops in Havasupai (see the Appendix). Watch for his photo tips throughout this guide.

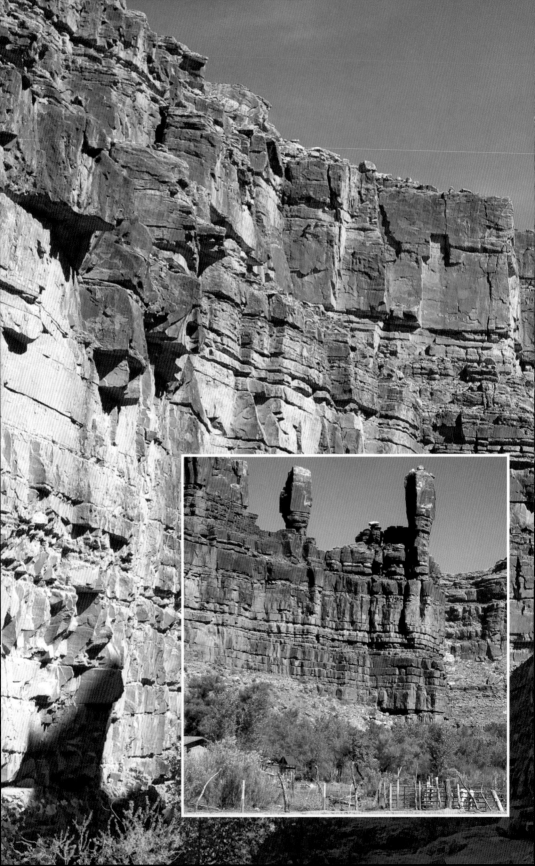

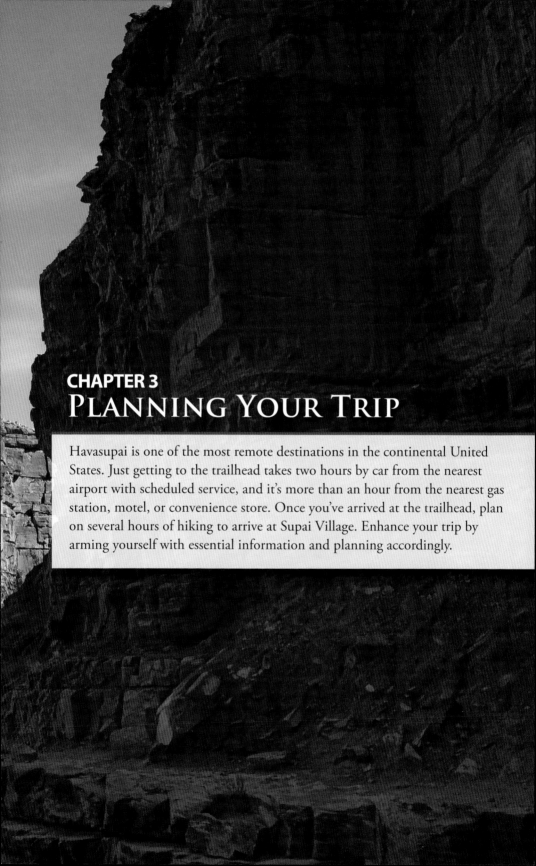

CHAPTER 3
PLANNING YOUR TRIP

Havasupai is one of the most remote destinations in the continental United States. Just getting to the trailhead takes two hours by car from the nearest airport with scheduled service, and it's more than an hour from the nearest gas station, motel, or convenience store. Once you've arrived at the trailhead, plan on several hours of hiking to arrive at Supai Village. Enhance your trip by arming yourself with essential information and planning accordingly.

PHYSICAL CONDITIONING

Exploring Havasupai is an active outdoor adventure that can be enjoyed by people of all ages with a wide range of physical abilities. Being in good physical condition will enable you to do more and have more fun.

A round-trip hike to the campground, including a visit to the major falls, can easily add up to 30 miles of hiking. While Havasupai may not have the elevation descent and gain associated with other Grand Canyon rim-to-river hikes, it has demanding terrain and the same heat, which can exact a physical toll.

Before you decide to hike to Havasupai, you should have some experience with hikes of a similar length and under similar conditions. Other hikes in the Grand Canyon, Colorado Plateau, or throughout the Southwest can provide a good comparative experience.

The great benefit of Havasupai is the availability of pack mules and saddle horses to lighten your load or even take you in and out on horseback. With the mules carrying a 30-pound pack, most active adults (even if a bit out of shape) will find hiking the trail challenging but doable. It's not uncommon to see children under age 10 and adults over 70 walking the trail alongside college students and experienced hikers.

WHEN TO GO

AVERAGE HIGH TEMPERATURES

	Jan	Feb	Mar	Apr	May	June	
°F	53°	61°	68°	76°	86°	96°	
°C	11°	15°	19°	24°	29°	35°	
	July	Aug	Sep	Oct	Nov	Dec	year
°F	100°	97°	90°	78°	64°	54°	77°
°C	37°	36°	32°	25°	17°	12°	24°

AVERAGE LOW TEMPERATURES

	Jan	Feb	Mar	Apr	May	June	
°F	28°	33°	38°	44°	52°	61°	
°C	-2°	0°	3°	6°	11°	15°	
	July	Aug	Sep	Oct	Nov	Dec	year
°F	66°	64°	57°	46°	36°	29°	46°
°C	18°	17°	13°	8°	2°	-1°	7°

AVERAGE HIGH PRECIPITATION

	Jan	Feb	Mar	Apr	May	June	
in.	0.6	0.6	0.9	0.4	0.4		
cm.	1	1	3	1	1	1	

	July	Aug	Sep	Oct	Nov	Dec	year
in.	1.2	1.4	0.7	0.6	0.7	0.8	8.5
cm.	3	3	2	1	2	2	21

AVERAGE HIGH SNOWFALL

	Jan	Feb	Mar	Apr	May	June	
in.	0.4	0.2	0	0	0	0	
cm.	1	0.5	0	0	0	0	

	July	Aug	Sep	Oct	Nov	Dec	year
in.	0	0	0	0	0.1	0.6	1.2
cm.	0	0	0	0	0	1.5	3

Because of its deep canyon setting and lower elevation, Havasupai has warmer weather than what you might find on the rim above. As a result, Havasupai draws a steady stream of visitors from March through mid-November.

Spring is the busiest time of the year as the campground swells with spring break (various weeks in late March and April) and Memorial Day weekend (last weekend in May) crowds. Spring is also popular with the many European tourists who come to Havasupai as part of an extended holiday in the American Southwest. The high sun and green foliage make May and June an ideal time for photography. Advance reservations are required.

Summer daytime temperatures hover in the high 90s, with canyon walls and cotton-wood providing welcome shade. The campground is filled with families, Scouts, and youth groups. Advance reservations are highly recommended.

In the sweltering heat, the creek and pools are especially refreshing. Trail temperatures during summer can be extreme, reaching 110°F. Plan your hiking to avoid the midday sun by departing the Hilltop trailhead well before dawn. On the exit, you can get a predawn start or wait until the late-afternoon shade provides some protection. In the summer it's not uncommon to see hikers with headlamps starting their final ascent to Hilltop after dark.

July, August, and early September are considered monsoon season in the Grand Canyon. Afternoon showers are common and the risk of flooding increases. Normally the storms are brief and refreshing and don't seem to limit activities or dampen anyone's spirits.

Fall is an ideal time to enjoy comfortable outdoor weather without crowds. After Labor Day weekend (first Monday in September), the younger visitors return to school and the campground demographics become decidedly grayer. You'll frequently share the trail with hikers in their 60s and 70s. International visitors also abound.

Winter is a quiet season in Havasupai. Steam rises from the relatively warm creek water, and days are short. Snow may dust the higher cliffs but rarely makes its way to the valley floor and never sticks. Water play isn't too attractive, but you don't have to worry about the midday sun on the Havasupai Trail, and it's still possible to enjoy the mesa and dry canyon hikes during the shorter days. Solitude at the waterfalls is a rare and wonderful winter gift.

MAKING RESERVATIONS

CAMPING RESERVATIONS During the March through October tourist season, the Havasupai Campground requires advance reservations. The Tourist Office does not start approving camping reservations until the first week in February. You'll find information about camping online at theofficialhavasupaitribe.com. To make reservations, call the Tourist Office in Supai at 928-448-2141 or 928-448-2121. For groups of 10 or more, call 928-448-2180.

When calling for reservations, you'll need to identify your desired dates, number of nights of camping, and the number of people in your party. You may secure the reservation by credit card. When you arrive in the village, stop at the Tourist Office to check in.

LODGE RESERVATIONS The lodge offers 24 rooms, each with two double beds, private bath, and air-conditioning. All rooms are nonsmoking. To make reservations, call 928-448-2111 or 928-448-2201.

When calling for reservations, you'll need to provide your contact information, arrival date, departure date, and credit card information to hold the reservation. When you arrive in the village, you can go straight to the lodge for check-in.

SADDLE AND PACK HORSE RESERVATIONS Arrangements for saddle or pack horses must be made in advance through the Tourist Office. One-way inbound arrangements must be made prior to arrival so that the appropriate number of horses is ready and waiting for you when you arrive. One-way outbound arrangements can be made in person at the Tourist Office at least a day prior to your departure date.

Horse reservations can be made by calling the Tourist Office at 928-448-2111 or 928-448-2201. You may also call the packers office directly at 928- 448-2237. The full amount is required in advance to guarantee reservations.

MAILING YOUR PACK

Many visitors to Havasupai choose to send their backpacks and other supplies by mail rather than carry them down the canyon. Although it takes advance planning, it's easier and less expensive than you might think. Simply take the unboxed backpack to your local U.S. post office. Allow a few extra days for delivery because Supai's mule mail operates just five days a week and often involves some extra delivery time. Attach a clearly visible luggage tag or label to the pack with the following address:

Your Name (Arrival Date)
General Delivery
Supai, AZ 86435

When you arrive in the village, just stop by the post office to pick up your pack. You'll still have to carry it the remaining 2 miles to the campground (unless you're staying in the lodge), but you've saved yourself 8 miles of backpacking, conserving your energy for day hikes and exploring the falls and canyons.

On your return, simply stop by the post office and label your pack for the return shipment home. Make sure you set aside a fanny pack or small hydration pack so you can carry sufficient water and snacks to get safely out of the canyon and back to the trailhead—and don't make the mistake of leaving your car keys in your pack at the post office.

WHAT TO PACK

GEAR For many backpackers, the essential question is always how much stuff to carry. With packhorses available to carry you and/or your gear directly to the campground, that question isn't a concern, but the cost is. However, if you're a purist and insist on hiking in with everything you need in your pack, you can still get by with a surprisingly light load. Don't stuff your pack with too much gear. By taking the minimalist approach, you'll be more comfortable and have just as much fun—maybe more.

Most Havasupai campers bring a lightweight tent for protection against the occasional rain shower and for storage and privacy in the campground. Others choose to sleep under the stars. For most of the year, a lightweight sleeping bag is ideal, while in midsummer a light fleece blanket or sleeping bag liner is all you will need. Hammocks are also a popular sleeping option in summer. Most hammocks can be compacted into a grapefruit-size ball and successfully replace bulkier sleeping bags, tents, and pads.

No campfires are allowed in the campground, so plan on cooking your meals over a campstove. Ultralight campers often prefer to leave the stove and fuel at home and to eat just cold food or snacks. If you don't mind the hike into the village, you can eat at the café or buy your food at the grocery store.

PLAN AHEAD

Quite simply, Havasupai is one of the most beautiful places on earth. The warm red sandstone walls, lush green foliage, and azure blue waters combine to produce some of the most richly saturated colors you'll ever see in a natural setting. One might think all you have to do to capture a great photograph is to point and shoot. You will get far more satisfying results if you plan ahead with equipment suited to the task.

—*Derek von Briesen*

Don't bother bringing your fishing gear to Havasupai. Other than a few minnows, there are no fish in Havasu Creek. From 1927 until the 1970s, trout were stocked in the creek above Havasu Falls, but they were repeatedly washed downstream in floods. Although the water is cold enough to support trout, some biologists have claimed the carbonates leave a film on the surface of the eggs, hampering fertilization. For whatever reason—floods, falls, or fertilization—fishing in Havasu Creek is a fruitless endeavor.

CLOTHES For the trail, plan on clothing that provides adequate sun protection, including a hat with a full brim. If you plan on spending a lot of time in the water—which most visitors do—you can get by with just a T-shirt and shorts around camp. If you're planning a longer hike to Beaver Falls or the Colorado River, you will probably want long pants to protect your legs while scrambling cliffs and picking your way around vines, thickets, and cacti.

SHOES The success of your trip will depend to a large extent on the footwear you choose. The 11-mile hike into the canyon will be a test of your shoes and your feet. For the trail, most hikers choose a light-duty, low-cut trail shoe. As your pack weight increases, you might gravitate toward the firmer midsole and the ankle support of a hiking boot, but for most of the Havasupai Trail, a lighter, more comfortable hiking shoe is the clear preference.

Once you hit the water you'll need river sandals or aqua socks with a firm, nonskid sole. In addition to playing in the waterfalls and pools, you will encounter frequent river crossings on any of the hikes below Mooney Falls, so a river sandal that's also well suited to hiking may be a good choice. Try them out on a short hike before you go. There's nothing worse than ill-fitting or poorly suited footwear that causes blisters.

In place of river sandals, some people bring a pair of old tennis shoes that they don't mind getting wet. Others wear socks with their sandals; it's not much of a fashion statement, but it is a good option for hiking and creek crossings. Just remember, you need to get yourself out of the canyon eventually, so keep your feet in good shape for the return.

WHAT TO BRING: A CHECKLIST

Essentials

Backpack

Bathing suit

Electrolyte replacement

First-aid kit

Food

Hat with brim

Headlamp or flashlight

Hiking shoes and socks

Personal toiletries, biodegradable soap

Refillable water containers (2 liters minimum)

Resealable plastic bags for packing out trash

River sandals or aqua socks

Sleeping bag or bag liner

Sleeping pad

Small towel

Sunscreen

Optional

Camera	Matches or lighter
Campstove and fuel	Notebook, pen, reading material
Cooking utensils, pots	Nylon cord, duct tape
Day pack	Pocketknife
Eating utensils, cup, bowl	Sunglasses
Extra batteries	Tent or tarp
Guidebook	Toilet paper
Hammock	Topo maps
Hiking poles	Trowel
Hiking shorts	Watch, compass, GPS device
Insect repellent	Water filter or tablets
Lightweight raingear	Wet suit
Lip balm	Whistle

WATER Drinking water is available in the village at the Tourist Office and in the campground at the spring. Bottled water and beverages can be purchased in the village during normal retail operating hours. Be sure to bring an adequate supply of drinking water with you to the trailhead.

Hiking in the desert requires careful planning and preparation. Hiking in extreme temperatures and dry air can quickly lead to dehydration. You should always carry water with you when hiking any Havasupai trail. When hiking the main trail from Hilltop to the village, start out well hydrated and carry at least two liters per person. Balance your water intake with electrolytes. Avoid hiking in direct sunlight and midday heat.

While the water in Havasu Creek flows clear and pure at a high volume, it is subject to contamination by horses, humans, and other mammals along the way, especially in the campground. Before you drink creek water you should purify it by boiling, or by using a water purifier or purification tablets. Water from other natural springs in the canyon is generally safe at the source, but purifying it will always give you an extra measure of protection.

Photo courtesy of iStock©stellgp

FOOD Havasupai offers hungry visitors a wide range of options, and you'll see many different preferences in the campground, from ultralight to ultraluxe.

Those who want to travel fast and light may choose to leave the stove at home and not cook at all. They get by just fine on snack foods, bagels, jerky, and fresh fruit. They may choose to supplement their snack items with some purchases at the general store or with a Supai taco from the café—but remember, these establishments are a 45-minute walk from the campground.

Most people bring along a backpacking stove or canister stove. Some prepare fancy camp cuisine, but most are just boiling water and eating oatmeal for breakfast and the popular freeze-dried backpacking meals for dinner. These meals are not available at the Supai store, so you must plan ahead and bring them with you. They are lightweight, easy to prepare, require little cleanup, and result in minimal waste to carry out. Beef Stroganoff, pasta primavera, sweet-and-sour pork—the options are pretty tasty.

Those who want to really live it up can have a full camp kitchen, including coolers, brought in on packhorses. It's not uncommon to see a family group or Scout troop with an elaborate meal plan. They start the day with bacon and eggs and come back to camp for steaks on the grill—a nice treat after a long day of hiking.

Regardless of what food you choose to bring, you need to plan on packing out all of your trash (including peelings, bones, wrappers, and containers). Campfires are not permitted, so you can't plan on just throwing your trash in the fire. You may want to skip the canned foods and unnecessary packaging. Plan your meals carefully and don't overpack.

SPECIAL CONSIDERATIONS REGARDING USE OF TRIBAL LANDS

The Havasupai tribe, like all other Native American tribes, has a nation-within-a-nation status. The term "tribal sovereignty" refers to the authority of a tribe to govern itself. Native American land is held in trust by the United States, and tribes have the power to control entry and manage use of tribal lands.

Visitors to Havasupai enter the canyon as guests of the Havasupai people. Guests are asked to observe the following rules:

- Alcoholic beverages are not permitted on the Havasupai Reservation. Illicit drugs are as illegal in Havasu Canyon as they are anywhere else.

- Tribal law does not permit the bearing of firearms by anyone on the reservation, nor are machetes necessary or useful in the campgrounds.

- Drones are not permitted in Havasupai.

- Gathering firewood is not permitted. No campfires are permitted in the campground or in other areas of the canyon.

- Havasupai does not accept the National Parks Pass, Eagle Pass, or other federal or state entrance and use programs.

- Please respect fences, private property, and the privacy of the people who call Havasu Canyon home.

- Due to the large number of animals living in Havasu Canyon (including wild predators and free-roaming dogs and horses), the tribe requests that visitors not bring pets with them.

HIKING WITH CHILDREN

Havasupai is a great family vacation destination, with activities and outdoor adventures that children love. There's something about playing under a waterfall or jumping into an effervescent pool that brings out the child in everyone.

With all the fun come some obvious risks—steep ledges, turbulent water, and uneven creek bottoms—which require close parental supervision, especially with young children. In addition, parents need to be alert for early signs of sunburn, hypothermia, dehydration, and blisters, as children normally do not recognize symptoms themselves. In fact, many adults don't recognize the symptoms until it's too late.

Most children over the age of 8 who are active and healthy will have little problem with the trail. Parents should distribute the gear so that children aren't carrying a load disproportionate to their weight. A 30-pound pack would be considered light for most adult males, but for an 80-pound preteen it would be absolute misery. Most adults carry the weight of a backpack on their hips, but most children haven't yet developed the hips to carry a backpack, and so the weight ends up being carried on their slender shoulders. A day pack with water and snacks is plenty for most children. Far better is to have a mule carry the load and allow young children to come away with a positive and memorable experience.

 CAMERA: CHANGING SETTINGS

For maximum effect, you'll need to control your camera's shutter speed by shrinking the lens opening (aperture and f/stops). Remember, the higher the f/stop number, the longer the exposure. Experiment and see what works best for the effect you want.
—*Derek von Briesen*

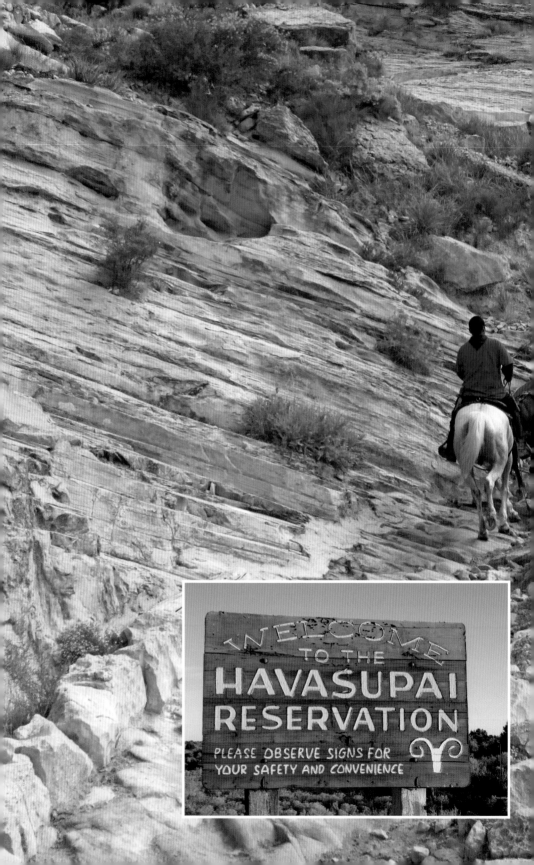

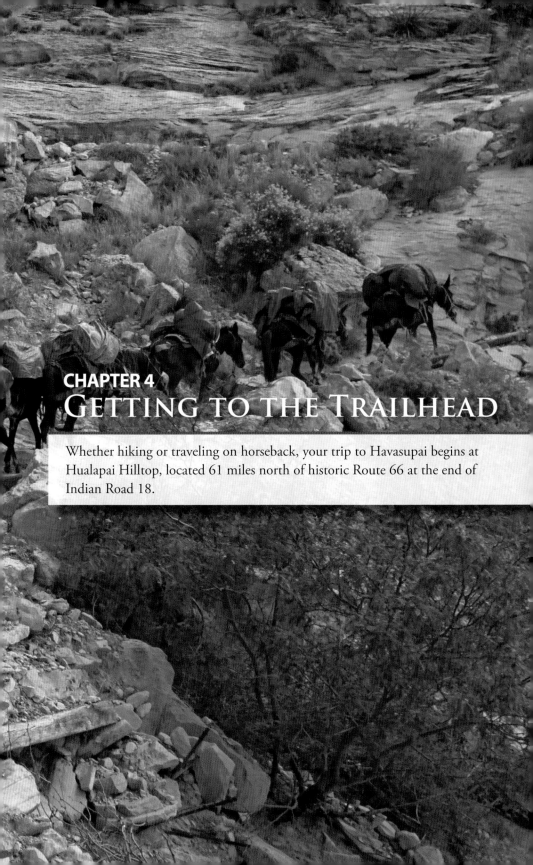

CHAPTER 4
GETTING TO THE TRAILHEAD

Whether hiking or traveling on horseback, your trip to Havasupai begins at
Hualapai Hilltop, located 61 miles north of historic Route 66 at the end of
Indian Road 18.

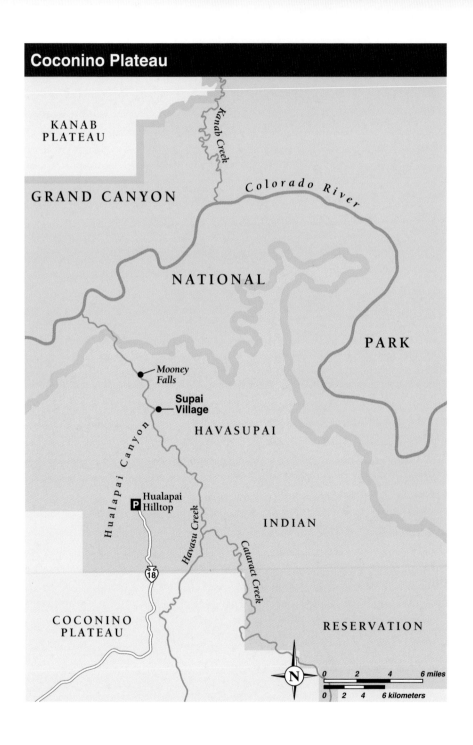

Coconino Plateau

KANAB
PLATEAU

Kanab Creek

GRAND CANYON

Colorado River

NATIONAL

PARK

Mooney
Falls

Supai
Village

HAVASUPAI

Hualapai Canyon

Hualapai
Hilltop

Havasu Creek

INDIAN

Cataract Creek

COCONINO
PLATEAU

RESERVATION

N

| 0 | 2 | 4 | 6 miles |
| 0 | 2 | 4 | 6 kilometers |

TRAVELING TO HUALAPAI HILLTOP

From Kingman, Arizona

If you're driving to Havasupai from the west (Las Vegas or Southern California), Kingman is your last stop for a full range of reliable services, groceries, or accommodations. From Kingman, the junction of Indian Road 18 is 54 miles to the east on Route 66. Along the way you will find a motel and gas station in Truxton, and a motel in Peach Springs, the headquarters of the Hualapai tribe. The Indian Road 18 junction is located 7 miles east of Peach Springs on Route 66. Plan on two to two and a half hours' driving time from Kingman to Hualapai Hilltop.

From Williams, Arizona

If you're driving to Havasupai from the south or east (Phoenix, Flagstaff, or Grand Canyon National Park), Williams is your likely gateway, and Seligman, located 30 miles east of the Indian Road 18 junction on Route 66, is your last stop for a full range of reliable services. There is also a gas station with 24-hour service and accommodations at Grand Canyon Caverns, just 5 miles east of Indian Road 18.

Indian Road 18

The junction for Indian Road 18 is located 7 miles east of Peach Springs and 5 miles west of Grand Canyon Caverns on Route 66. Before you turn off Route 66 onto Indian Road 18, make sure you have sufficient gas for the 137 round-trip miles of driving and enough water for your hike into the canyon. There are no services of any kind (gas, water, food, flush toilets, or lodging) on Indian Road 18 or at the Hualapai Hilltop parking area.

No lighting, little signage, and few reflective markers make Indian Road 18 challenging after dark. Fortunately, the two-lane road is paved the entire way from Route 66 to Hilltop.

Indian Road 18 rolls and winds over a high desert plateau dotted with juniper, sage, and at higher elevations, broad forests of ponderosa pine. You may see more wildlife along this road than in the canyon. Particularly in the evening hours, elk and mule deer are commonly sighted along the road, as are coyotes, bobcats, and jackrabbits.

The road stays within the Hualapai Reservation for 40 miles before entering a short stretch of private and state trust lands. Near milepost 52 there are some high elevation points along the road that offer sweeping views extending to the north rim of the Grand Canyon and beyond.

Just past milepost 55 you enter the Havasupai Reservation. Shortly after entering the reservation, at milepost 57, the road begins a winding descent down a wash through outcroppings of Toroweap formation. Free-grazing horses are frequently on the road both day and night, so drive carefully. The Hualapai Hilltop trailhead parking area is at mile 61 at the end of Indian Road 18.

Other Roads to Hualapai Hilltop

The series of interconnected unpaved roads that crisscross the Coconino Plateau between Grand Canyon National Park and the Havasupai Reservation are a poor choice for accessing Havasupai. One road, number 306, begins 7 miles south of the entrance to the park on State Highway 64 and connects with Indian Road 18 about 7 miles south of Hualapai Hilltop. These roads are rough at best and often require a high-clearance, four-wheel-drive vehicle. In some stretches you'll only average 5 to 10 mph. To make matters worse, some private landowners have gated or closed the road entirely, which results in backtracking and uncertain access. Do not consider navigating this network of tracks without detailed maps.

INTO THE CANYON

From Hilltop to Supai

Although there are no camping facilities at the Hilltop parking area, many summer hikers arrive late at night, then sleep in their cars or on a pad by the side of the road, and hit the trail before sunrise. Others choose to arrive at Hilltop late in the afternoon and make an evening arrival in Supai. Staying in Peach Springs or at Grand Canyon Caverns and driving to the Hilltop trailhead before dawn is another option. To avoid hiking in the heat of the summer, plan your departure based on your hiking speed, sunrise and sunset times, temperature forecasts, and the possibility of a protective cloud cover. A detailed guide to hiking into the canyon is found in Chapter 12, pages 73–81.

Saddle and Pack Services

By making advance arrangements you can ride a horse to the campground or lodge, or hike in and have a horse carry your gear. Many groups choose to hike in and arrange for one mule among the group to lighten the load. Other groups put the younger, older, or less fit members on horses, while the better-conditioned hikers hit the trail on foot. But be aware that unless you have riding experience and a good seat, you may be more comfortable walking. Having saddle and packhorses available gives you plenty of options so that visitors of all ages and physical capabilities can enjoy Havasupai.

Pack train in Hualapai Canyon

SADDLE HORSES To ride a horse to Supai you should have a basic level of riding experience and be able to mount, dismount, and guide the horse unassisted. You must be at least 4'7" and must not weigh more than 250 pounds. You can carry a small day pack (less than 20 pounds), a camera, and a water container. Riders are not allowed to carry backpacks on a riding horse.

An adult is permitted to ride with a child 5 years of age or younger, and the total weight cannot exceed 250 pounds.

Riders should wear long pants, a long-sleeved shirt, and a large-brimmed hat, cap, or visor to be most comfortable.

Horses are owned by individual tribal packers and must be brought up from the village, so be sure to confirm your horse reservations a day before traveling to Hilltop. Those bringing their own horses pay a trail fee and must provide their own feed.

PACK MULES A pack mule will carry up to four articles with a combined maximum weight of 130 pounds. Articles going on the mule should be of proportionate size and weight to maintain balance and to achieve easier packing. The maximum bag size is 36 inches long, 19 inches wide, and 16 inches tall. Duffel bags are highly recommended. Expensive luggage is discouraged. Ice chests must not exceed 48-quart capacity, and dimensions must not exceed 24 inches long by 19 inches wide. Even though the packers make every effort to deliver your bags in the condition they were received, the packing ropes and the constant movement of the horses may cause wear and tear.

Bags must be individually tagged for identification and checked in with the tour coordinator at the Hilltop trailer. A coordinator can be found as early as 7 a.m. If the coordinator is not available and you wish to make an early start, you can leave your baggage with night security. If neither is available for assistance, stay with your bags until someone arrives to assist you. Do not leave your bags unattended.

When returning from the campground to Hilltop, set your tagged bags at the entrance of the campground for pickup.

MULE TRAIN SCHEDULE Mule trains depart Hualapai Hilltop daily between 10 a.m. and noon and arrive at the campground by 3:30 p.m. The mule train will wait for any late arrivals until noon. If you arrive after noon, you will forfeit your mule reservation and deposit.

Mule trains depart the campground at 7 a.m. (April through October) or 8 a.m. (November through March) and reach Hilltop between 10 a.m. and noon. Mule trains depart the lodge at 8 a.m. year-round.

Helicopter Services

Airwest Helicopters provides passenger and freight helicopter service between Hualapai Hilltop and Supai Village. From March 15 to October 15, service is provided four days per week on Sunday, Monday, Thursday, and Friday. During the off-season, from October 15 to March 15, service is provided only on Friday and Sunday. Flights operate from 10 a.m. to 1 p.m. on service days.

Helicopter landing in Supai

There are no reservations, and service is offered on a first-come, first-served basis. Tribal members have first priority, followed by teachers, consultants and contractors on tribal business, and finally tourists. But as long as you check in during the service hours, you should be able to make it aboard that day.

There are always those who make it down into the canyon, then realize they don't have the stamina or capability to make it out under their own power. For those individuals, just knowing the helicopter is available provides a viable backup plan or "escape route."

You may carry one medium-size bag or backpack onboard for free. All other cargo is billed as freight. Airwest can also haul up to 700 pounds of swing load freight. Pets can be flown. Children under the age of 2 fly for free. For additional information, rates, and schedule updates contact Airwest Helicopters at 623-516-2790 or online at airwesthelicopters.com.

CHAPTER 5
HAVASUPAI HISTORY

EARLY HISTORY

In a canyon with exposed rock dating back more than 1.8 billion years, the significance of any human history—even for a people who have been on the scene for the past 1,000 years or so—almost pales in relation to the canyon's geologic history. When Columbus set sail for the new world in 1492, the Havasupai people had already been living in their Havasu Canyon home for hundreds of years. Before their arrival in Havasu Canyon, the Havasupai were likely part of the Yuman-speaking Pai Indians, whose traditional lands included much of the lower Colorado River valley and adjacent areas in what is now southern California, western Arizona, and northern Baja California. The Pai are part of a larger Hokan group of people who are believed to have inhabited the area for 30,000 years.

For centuries, movement with the seasons dictated the location of the Havasupai. In summer they built brush-and-mud-covered shelters known as *wickiups* on the floor of Havasu Canyon. Here they irrigated their staple crops of corn, squash, and beans and wove baskets. After the August harvest they moved to the cooler but sun-drenched upper plateau, where they successfully hunted deer, elk, bighorn sheep, and smaller animals. While wintering on the plateau, they built wickiups and became expert in the tanning of hides. In early spring they would return to the inner canyon, continuing a cycle that offered reliable sustenance in a region where a sedentary lifestyle would have been unsustainable.

The Grand Canyon

"The Grand Canyon discovered in 1540 by Pedro de Cardenas" the National Parks pamphlet read. I smiled knowing that my people always knew the Grand Canyon was there and didn't need to be discovered.

—*Michael Kabotie (Lomawywesa)*

Hopi artist and poet

While Captain Garcia Lopez de Cardenas, part of Francisco Coronado's 1540 expedition, is believed to have been the first European to see the Grand Canyon, it's unlikely he ever encountered the Havasupai people or Havasu Canyon. That occurred in 1776 when Francisco Garcés, a Franciscan missionary, explored the area and found the Havasupai, whom he observed as friendly and hospitable and already in possession of horses. He called the creek Rio Jabesua, a Spanish adaptation of "Havasu," and left without any converts.

In 1867 an indomitable one-armed Civil War veteran and scientist, John Wesley Powell, left his professorship in geology at Illinois Wesleyan University to explore the American West. In his epic 1867 expedition down the Colorado River he explored Havasu Canyon, which he named Coanini Creek, and suggested it had its headwaters in the San Francisco Mountain to the south. In Powell's wake came cattlemen, miners, and other settlers to the region, forcing the Havasupai into a diminishing and restricted area within Havasu Canyon. By 1880, U.S. President Rutherford B. Hayes established a reservation for the Havasupai about 12 miles long and 5 miles wide along the corridor of Havasu Creek.

Havasupai building trails in Grand Canyon National Park (1932)

CONFINED TO THE CANYON

By 1882, under pressure from mining and cattle interests, the total area of the reservation was surveyed and established with just 518 acres, less than a square mile, an area roughly defined by the present-day Supai Village. Cattlemen now occupied the Havasupai's winter range, and miners were given claim to tracts along Havasu Creek in the area of Havasu and Mooney Falls. Instantly, hundreds of square miles of traditional Havasupai homelands and range became public property, no longer usable by the Havasupai people. The Havasupai, who used to roam freely between the sheltered canyon and plateau expanses were now perennially confined to a small tract of land ill-suited to their traditional way of life. That sense of confinement is still felt by the tribe today.

Beyond the constraints of adapting to a new way of life without access to their traditional hunting grounds, the Havasupai faced two cataclysmic events in the early 20th century that decimated, and nearly eliminated, the tribe. Although summer rains and occasional flooding are always a risk in the canyon, the freak winter flood of 1910 was the most damaging flood ever recorded in Supai. Unusually heavy snowfall in December 1909 blanketed the plateau around Christmas. A sudden thaw and heavy rains on New Year's Day sent a 20-foot wall of water charging down the canyon shortly before dawn on January 2. In addition to loss of human life, much livestock was lost, and every house in Supai Village was destroyed, as was the stone

Original Havasupai School built in 1895 and destroyed in the 1910 flood (1899)

schoolhouse. At that time the village was located near the confluence of Hualapai and Havasu canyons, farther south than the present-day village, and the farmlands, which lay farther down the canyon, were washed away and filled with debris. In 1918 the tribe was struck by the influenza pandemic that killed between 20 and 40 million people worldwide. Its devastating impact on the Havasupai tribe was particularly damaging to families with young children. Some families lost all of their children within a span of a few weeks, and tribal population dropped well below its historical level of 250 members.

The creation of Grand Canyon National Park in 1919 formalized the jurisdiction of the land surrounding the small Havasupai tract. Many Havasupai men were employed to build the Bright Angel Trail and other trail and construction projects within the park and were housed in a camp near the railroad station at the South Rim. One Havasupai man, known as Burro, continued to farm his plot at Indian Garden below the South Rim until 1928, when he was eventually chased out of the canyon. Throughout this period, the plight of the Havasupai, their inability to occupy and use traditional lands, and their isolation within the confines of their reservation became a source of bitterness and contention.

TRIBAL LAND RESTORED

In 1975, after more than 60 years of petitions, claims, proposals, and counterproposals to regain its traditional lands, the Havasupai tribe was granted by U.S. Congress

185,000 acres of land adjacent and to the south of Grand Canyon National Park. The enactment of this legislation increased the size of the Havasupai tribal lands from less than 1 square mile to more than 276 square miles. It was the largest amount of land ever restored to a single tribe and included not only the waterfalls and canyon lands as far north as Beaver Canyon but also large stretches of Cataract Canyon and Hualapai Canyon to the south of the village and significant expanses of Topocoba Plateau and Great Thumb Mesa to the east. The return of these lands to the tribe was a landmark fulfillment of generations of Havasupai dreams, struggles, and aspirations.

Today, the Havasupai are the only indigenous people who continue to live in the Grand Canyon. Beginning in the 1960s and growing steadily into the present, the Havasupai have developed an economic base of sustainable tourism. Most jobs and tribal revenue are derived from tourist services, including packing, accommodations, camping, and retail operations in the village.

Although their traditional lands have been restored to them, it's unlikely that the Havasupai people will ever return to their traditional way of life.

Manakaja

Chief Manakaja was the last chief of the Havasupai before they converted to a tribal council form of government in 1934. He was, and remains, a legendary figure among the Havasupai, standing as a bridge between a time when the tribe called the plateau their home and the period in which they were confined to the canyon floor. As a young man, Manakaja roamed the expanse of Havasupai land and lived off the earth. During his tenure as chief

of the Havasupai tribe he led the fight to have those lands restored to his people. He occupied his position as chief from 1900 until his death in 1942. While he never lived to see the restoration of his tribe's land, the enactment of the legislation in 1975 was due in large part to his persistent efforts.

Manakaja, last chief of the Havasupai

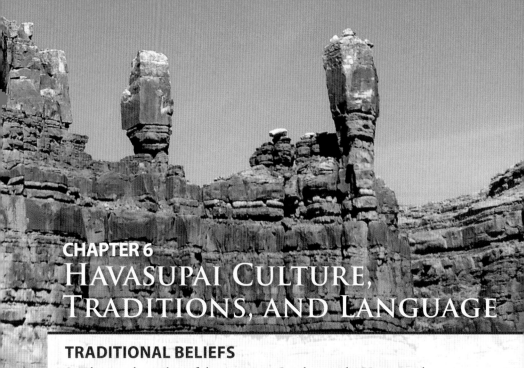

CHAPTER 6
HAVASUPAI CULTURE, TRADITIONS, AND LANGUAGE

TRADITIONAL BELIEFS

Similar to other tribes of the American Southwest, the Havasupai have a naturalistic body of traditional belief that encompasses and defines the world around them. They regard Mother Earth as a living, breathing being; the springs and creeks that fill the canyon are her bloodstream. Because she gives life to the canyon, the Havasupai people show respect for the earth and view the canyon and its life-giving water as sacred. Because they respect the earth, the earth's resources will hear, guide, and protect the Havasupai.

The Havasupai call the canyon their grandmother, and its various layers, especially the red rocks, have special significance for them. The rocks of the canyon protect the Havasupai and their way of life. Since the Havasupai are the only natives living inside the canyon, they regard themselves as the guardians of the canyon and all that lies below the rim.

The Seasoned Guide

In 1941, this 4-year-old Havasupai boy (see photo below) was sent by his parents with his brother, age 6, to guide a party of visitors up the 9-mile Havasupai Trail from Supai Village to Hilltop. Neither boy could speak English and neither could mount his horse without leading it to a ledge or a rock for a step. After successfully guiding their clients to the Hilltop trailhead, the boys expertly herded four unladen horses back down the canyon trail to their home in the village. (Photo courtesy Northern Arizona University).

AGRICULTURE

As you enter Supai Village you'll notice an irrigation channel running parallel to the creek. While the exact age of the irrigation system is unknown, it is believed to be more than 200 years old. The system consists of two channels that run on both sides

of the creek as it passes through the village. Over time, the system has been expanded and fitted with updated diversion gates.

The Havasupai have a strong agricultural tradition and were widely recognized as the best farmers among the tribes in the area. They were self-reliant through much of the 20th century, and their ancient irrigation system suggests that they had been so throughout most of their history in the canyon. While hunting was a role reserved for males, farming was a shared responsibility by both male and female members of the tribe.

The Bible in Havasupai

Once Havasupai became a written language, work began on a Bible translation. In 1979, Scott and Lynanne Palmer, with Wycliffe Bible Translators, came to Supai to begin the lengthy process of translating the New Testament and parts of Genesis into Havasupai.

The translation of a section begins with Scott and native speaker Bemus Uqualla reading the passage together. Study guides and written aids help them unlock meaning and gain a clear understanding of the passage. Then Bemus translates the passage into Havasupai.

The initial translation is then rigorously tested with people of various ages throughout the village. They translate, test, and translate again until the translated passage satisfies three criteria—it must be clear, accurate, and natural.

Scriptural translation poses a number of challenges. For example, the Havasupai language doesn't have much of a nautical vocabulary, so words like *rudder, mainsail anchor, or stern* present minor obstacles. But as translators come to challenging passages, they find that Havasupai is a descriptive language, fully capable of conveying the meaning of any text with clarity.

This ambitious undertaking is moving forward at a steady pace. Shortly, the project will be completed, giving the Havasupai people the opportunity to read the Bible in their own language.

HORSEMANSHIP

The Havasupai have been using horses since shortly after the Spanish explored the area in 1540. Throughout the later 18th century and into the 19th century they used horses in their seasonal travel to the plateau and in travel as they traded with other

Havasupai horsemen were among the state's top rodeo competitors (circa 1947).

tribes, especially the Hopi. Into the early 20th century the Havasupai became expert horsemen and were accustomed to taking top prizes at the Indian rodeos held throughout Arizona.

When it comes time to break a horse, the Havasupai have a simpler, far more sensible approach than western cowboys. They lead the horse out to a deep section of the stream, next to a large rock. Then the rider climbs from the rock onto the horse. In the deep water of the creek the horse is unable to buck and put up much of a fight. After a couple of days of repeating this process, the horse is broken and ready to ride.

Today, horse packing is the primary source of revenue for tribal members. The Havasupai take pride in the care and treatment of their horses. They have a farrier (a blacksmith or horseshoer) in the village, and most packers are proficient in hoof care and teach this craft to their children. Havasupai horsemanship is often displayed on the trail shared with hikers. Their balance and speed on unstable and uneven trail surfaces are evidence of their well-honed skills.

HAVASUPAI LANGUAGE

The Havasupai language is one of the Hokan languages, a family of languages spoken by indigenous peoples throughout the western United States and Mexico. Within the Hokan language family are nine Yuman languages spoken by tribes in western Arizona, Southern California, and Mexico's Baja California and Sonora. Some of these languages are still widely spoken among the population, while others have been dead for more than a hundred years or are spoken by just a few tribal elders.

Although Havasupai is spoken by fewer than 700 people, it remains a vibrant and actively spoken language. In fact, Havasupai is the only Native American language in the United States spoken by 100 percent of the tribal population. Like many indigenous languages, Havasupai existed only as a spoken language until the mid-1970s, when a written form was finally developed.

To the ear of most Americans, Havasupai is absolutely unfamiliar—but it has a soft, pleasant sound, without guttural resonance or the hard fricative consonants of English. Still, you're not likely to return home with any Havasupai vocabulary rolling off your tongue.

Havasupai is commonly spoken in the home and among tribal members in public. Schoolchildren can be heard playing and chatting in their native tongue. In the village you'll frequently hear locals talking among themselves in Havasupai and then seamlessly slipping into English as a courtesy to visitors.

Wigleeva and Havasu Canyon, as they appeared in 1899, before Supai Village was located in this part of the canyon

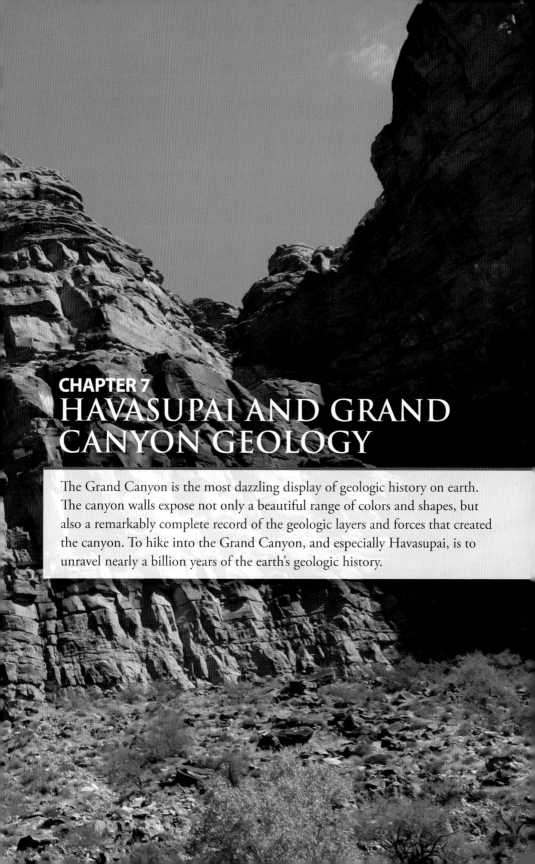

CHAPTER 7
HAVASUPAI AND GRAND CANYON GEOLOGY

The Grand Canyon is the most dazzling display of geologic history on earth. The canyon walls expose not only a beautiful range of colors and shapes, but also a remarkably complete record of the geologic layers and forces that created the canyon. To hike into the Grand Canyon, and especially Havasupai, is to unravel nearly a billion years of the earth's geologic history.

It was the geology of the Grand Canyon that first attracted the interest of John Wesley Powell, a professor of geology in Illinois, leading him to undertake his exploration of the canyon. Later, President Theodore Roosevelt relied on the geological attributes of the canyon, not its scenic or recreational potential, to declare it a national monument under the 1906 Antiquities Act.

Havasu Canyon offers visitors the benefit of being able to walk through the complete range of the dramatic rock layers that compose the Grand Canyon and come face to face with each layer. The flow of Havasu Creek, with its cycle of flooding and depositing of sediments, reminds us that the Grand Canyon is still a work in progress.

The Grand Canyon was carved through the sedimentary layers that comprise a vast area known as the Colorado Plateau. This plateau covers most of southern Utah, northern Arizona, southwestern Colorado, and northwestern New Mexico. The section of the Colorado Plateau that encompasses the south rim of Grand Canyon National Park and Havasu Canyon is known as the Coconino Plateau.

LUSCIOUS LAYERS

As you descend through the different geologic layers, note how the rock changes color and texture. The weathering from wind and water affects each layer differently, creating a variety of shapes. Watch for the changing scenery as you walk. With early morning or late afternoon lighting, the shadows can be deep and dramatic.

—*Derek von Briesen*

The sedimentary layers found in Havasu Canyon are similar to those throughout the Grand Canyon, both on the north and south rim. As the Colorado River and its tributaries cut through layers of rock, these layers are exposed and sculpted into distinctly identifiable slopes and cliffs found in the main canyon and throughout dozens of side canyons.

WHAT TO WATCH FOR

For the Havasupai visitor, the layers become instantly identifiable from the moment you leave the trailhead. The Hilltop trailhead is positioned on a cliff below the Kaibab and Toroweap formations. As you leave the parking area you are immediately immersed in a trail that cuts through the towering yellowish cliffs of Coconino sandstone, deposited 250 million years ago as windblown desert sand dunes. These exposed sandstone cliffs are one of the most recognizable and prominent features in the Grand Canyon.

About halfway down the steep trail from Hilltop to the floor of Hualapai Canyon, you'll notice that the color changes from yellow to red as you pass through a layer of Hermit shale. The Hermit formation is softer rock than the Coconino formation above or the Supai Group below, so it forms a gentler slope as it leads to the canyon floor.

As you walk down Hualapai Canyon toward Supai Village, you are surrounded by the reddish walls of the Supai Group. The Supai Group was deposited about 300 million years ago in swampy lowlands. The red stairsteps through Hualapai Canyon and the cliffs surrounding Supai Village are all part of the Supai Group.

The most prominent cliff layer in the Grand Canyon is the Redwall limestone formation, deposited in a shallow sea about 320 million years ago. The Redwall limestone is gray in color but is stained red by iron oxide washed from the red layers above. Interestingly, the Havasupai people refer to the Redwall layer as the "Graywall."

The Redwall layer begins at the village level and continues to below Mooney Falls. All of Havasupai's major waterfalls occur in the Redwall layer; this layer also forms the walls towering over the campground. Throughout the Grand Canyon the Redwall is a major barrier to travel, and some of the canyon's most dramatic and punishing trails make their steep descent through breaks in the Redwall.

Below Mooney Falls, you'll find Temple Butte and Mauv limestone, particularly noticeable as you descend the cliffs to access Beaver Falls. If you visit the Colorado River, you'll also have a chance to see Zoroaster Granite and 1.75-billion-year-old Vishnu Schist, some of the oldest exposed rock in America.

Towering cliffs above the canyon

Despite the age of the rock and sedimentary layers that make up the Grand Canyon, the canyon itself is relatively young. Everything visible from the canyon rim to the Colorado River was carved in the past 5 to 6 million years. And despite the visible changes that have occurred in this timeframe, the geology of the Colorado Plateau itself is stable, allowing the changes to be viewed and understood today.

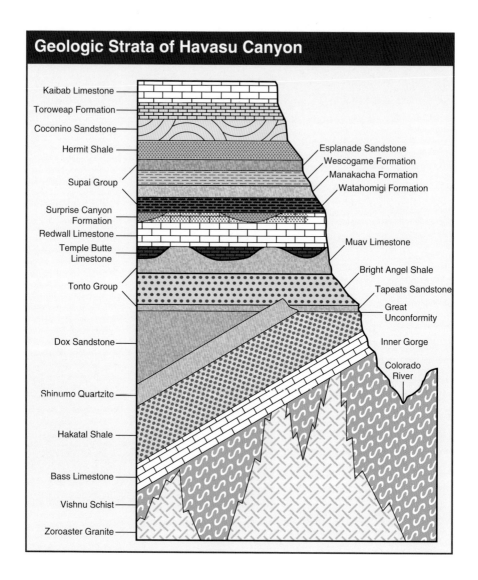

Geologic Strata of Havasu Canyon

Kaibab Limestone
Toroweap Formation
Coconino Sandstone
Hermit Shale
Supai Group
Surprise Canyon Formation
Redwall Limestone
Temple Butte Limestone
Tonto Group
Dox Sandstone
Shinumo Quartzite
Hakatal Shale
Bass Limestone
Vishnu Schist
Zoroaster Granite

Esplanade Sandstone
Wescogame Formation
Manakacha Formation
Watahomigi Formation
Muav Limestone
Bright Angel Shale
Tapeats Sandstone
Great Unconformity
Inner Gorge
Colorado River

WATER AND EROSION

While the creation of the Grand Canyon is generally seen as the work of the Colorado and other rivers flowing across the Colorado Plateau during the last 5 to 6 million years, the surface and form of the canyon have also been shaped by other forces. Water, and to a lesser extent, wind continue to carve the canyon walls. Freezing and warming of rocks creates cracks and fissures where water can enter and expand. Rock falls and slides move material closer to the canyon floor. Flash floods shape the side canyons in subtle ways and carry debris downstream into the Colorado River.

The ongoing forces of erosion are particularly active and visible in Havasupai. Flash floods have the effect of bursting some of the travertine rims from time to time. But as some rims are broken, others continue to form and build up. New Navajo Falls is one example of a waterfall that has changed dramatically in the last century, and particularly in 2008, because of flash flooding. The appearance of Havasu Falls has also changed considerably in recent years as its two columns became one broad column with the breaking of a center divider. Following the 2008 flood, its height dropped about five feet, and the direction of its flow shifted to the side.

Natural springs in the area also give life to the canyon. One official survey of the canyons on the Havasupai Reservation identified more than 50 springs. These springs can't compete with the 38 million gallons of water produced by Havasu Creek each day, but they do carve their own channels and nourish vegetation, which in turn can reduce surface erosion.

Wigleeva

The two pillars standing as sentinels over the western canyon wall above Supai Village are known as the Wigleeva. The Havasupai people look to the two towers, one male and the other female, as guardian figures over the village and its residents. The legend holds that when the towers fall, that will spell the end of the canyon and of the Havasupai people.

Wigleeva from Supai Village

CHAPTER 8
HAVASUPAI FLORA AND FAUNA

FLORA

PRICKLY PEAR *(Opuntia erinacea)* This is the most common of all cacti and can be found throughout Havasu Canyon. Its flat pads and jointed stems soak up and store water quickly in rainstorms and have the ability to self-prune and drop joints during dry years. The fruit of the prickly pear ripens in September and is eaten by the Havasupai.

MESQUITE *(Prosopis glandulosa)* This small tree or large shrub has a blackish bark, thorny branches, and small leaves. The hardy mesquite is well adapted to the harsh desert climate and can draw water through its long taproot, recorded to be as much as 190 feet deep. The beans from mesquite pods are rich in sugar, protein, and minerals and were often ground into meal by the Havasupai.

COYOTE WILLOW *(Salix exigua)* There are actually four species of willow in Havasu Canyon found in riparian thickets and throughout the canyon floor. With its long, narrow leaves, the coyote willow is known as a pioneering species, being one of the first to appear in gravelly and sandy flood deposits. It also adapts well to areas like Havasu Canyon that are flooded on a regular basis.

SHRUB LIVE OAK *(Quercus turbinella)* This shrub is found in Hualapai Canyon and other rocky dry canyons at middle elevations and above creek level. Leaves are oblong and stiff, with sharp lobes, similar to holly. The shrub live oak provides an important habitat and food source for Havasu Canyon's mammals, birds, and insects.

Cactus on West Mesa Trail

BARREL CACTUS *(Ferocactus)* This cactus is common on the desert mesas both above and below the Redwall. Most cacti in Havasu Canyon are between one and two feet tall, but this same slow-growing species can reach heights up to ten feet and live for more than 100 years. Don't fall for the myth that you can cut into the barrel cactus to obtain emergency drinking water. You'll get nothing but bitter juice and a damaged cactus.

COTTONWOOD *(Populus fremontii)* Cottonwood "likes to keep its feet wet," and its presence is always a sign of water nearby. This large spreading shade tree is found throughout the canyon floor, where its deep roots protect riparian soils from erosion. When the female cottonwood releases its downy seeds in the spring, Havasupai farmers know it's time to plant their corn.

BIG SAGEBRUSH *(Artemisia tridentata)* This iconic shrub of the southwest, with its gray-green, silvery leaves, is found throughout Havasu Canyon. Its aromatic oils make it a popular fuel in many Native American ceremonial fires. Those same oils also make it less desirable as a food source for deer, sheep, and elk.

Cactus flower

The sagebrush is used by the Havasupai as a cough suppressant. The related European species is known in American kitchens as tarragon.

BRITTLEBRUSH *(Encelia farinosa)* This small flowering scrub plant is common in all side canyons of the Grand Canyon. Its yellow flowers are found throughout the Havasu Canyon from spring through fall.

OCOTILLO *(Fouquieria splendens)* Often called "coach-whip," this shrub is not widely dispersed in Havasu Canyon, but when you see it, it's unmistakable. The ocotillo's thorny branches rise 6 to 10 feet high on desert mesas and in Hualapai Canyon. In the late spring its red blossoms attract hummingbirds.

Ocotillo

MORMON TEA *(Ephedra viridis)* Also known as joint-fir, this shrub with round, green, woody stems is actually related to the pine tree. Havasupai used Mormon tea to relieve coughs and nasal congestion. The plant contains pseudoephedrine, commonly used as a decongestant in over-the-counter medications.

Mormon tea on the West Mesa Trail

FAUNA

Mammals

COYOTE *(Canis latrans)* Coyotes are intelligent, social members of the dog family that hunt nocturnally in pairs or small family groups for deer, sheep, and rabbits. Found mainly on the higher plateaus, they can also be seen on lower mesas in Havasu Canyon. They have amazing stamina and adaptability to the desert environment. A coyote can sprint up to 40 mph and travel more than 200 miles in a night.

BIGHORN SHEEP *(Ovis canadensis)* Desert big-horn populations are increasing now that nonnative wild burros, the sheep's major competitor for limited desert food, have been removed from the Grand Canyon. They are best spotted in early morning on rocky cliffs around Beaver Canyon,

Desert bighorn roam Havasupai's high cliffs.

the West Mesa Trail, and the Apache Trail. When desert bighorn sheep make a rare appearance on the canyon floor, it is a traditional sign of ancestors communicating an important warning or message. The Havasupai recall desert bighorn sheep appearing in the village immediately prior to the attacks on September 11, 2001.

Elusive mountain lions have a home in Havasupai.

MOUNTAIN LION *(Felis concolor)* The mountain lion, also known as cougar, stands at the top of the Grand Canyon food chain. An adult cougar can weigh more than 200 pounds and measure 8 feet long. They can jump 20 to 30 feet, outrun a deer, and stalk their prey more than 25 miles in one night. Scat and paw prints can be found throughout the canyon, but the cat itself is rarely seen. Attacks on humans are rare.

GRAY FOX *(Urocyon cinereoargenteus)* Common on the floor and lower mesas of Havasu Canyon, the gray fox competes with the coyote for small prey such as rabbits and small rodents. It also eats prickly pear fruit and other garden crops in the canyon.

ELK *(Cervus elaphus)* The largest animal on the reservation, a bull elk sporting a full rack can weigh as much as 1,000 pounds. The elk found around the Grand Canyon today are Rocky Mountain elk, which were transplanted to the area between 1912 and 1967 after native elk were hunted to extinction. Elk sightings (and potential collisions) are common along Indian Road 18, south of the Havasupai Reservation.

Bull elk are abundant on the Coconino Plateau.

DESERT COTTONTAIL *(Sylvilagus audubonii)* This whitish-tan rabbit is found throughout the sage and cottonwood vegetation of Havasu Canyon. Females can produce 20 to 30 offspring per year, making cottontails an abundant food source for nearly every predator, including owls, rattlesnakes, coyotes, bobcats—and humans.

Desert cottontails hide in the underbrush of the canyon floor.

Birds

YELLOW WARBLER *(Dendroica petechia)* This distinctive songbird is common throughout the riparian regions of Havasu Canyon. Easily spotted by its yellow body as it nests in the willows of the campground, it feeds primarily on ground insects.

CANYON WREN *(Catherpes mexicanus)* More frequently heard than seen, this small wren is widely distributed throughout the western United States and Mexico but is particularly enjoyed in the Grand Canyon, as its familiar whistling call echoes across canyons. It builds its nests in rock crevices on dry canyon walls near water.

COMMON RAVEN *(Corvus corax)* This largest member of the crow family, about two feet long, can be seen year-round throughout Havasu Canyon. It is common in the village and around the campground. Ravens are among the most intelligent of birds. In spring, ravens perform aerial courtships and mate for life.

GREAT BLUE HERON *(Ardea herodias)* Watching one of these four-foot-long blue-gray birds take flight along Havasu Creek is more spectacular than watching a helicopter lift Porta Potties from the campground. Great blues are common below Mooney Falls and along the Colorado River. One of their greatest predators in the canyon is the eagle, which preys on chicks and can even take an adult heron.

BELTED KINGFISHER *(Ceryle alcyon)* The belted kingfisher is seen below Mooney Falls during spring and fall migrations. Recognized by its short legs, stocky body, white neck, and blue crown, it feeds on fish, so it rarely makes an appearance in the upper canyon.

BLACK-CHINNED HUMMINGBIRD *(Archilochus alexandri)* This blackish-green species is the most common of several hummingbirds found in the canyon. They nest in the canyon in spring and summer before returning to Mexico for the winter. The only bird able to fly backward, hummingbirds can fly at speeds up to 30 mph and beat their wings up to 50 times per second.

Reptiles

CALIFORNIA KING SNAKE *(Lampropeltis getulus)* Common throughout Havasu Canyon and in canyon bottoms throughout the Grand Canyon, the California king snake is easily identifiable by its black and white (or occasionally cream-colored) bands. It is called the king snake because it preys on other snakes, including venomous ones. Its presence in the canyon accounts for the scarcity of rattlesnakes. California king snakes can grow up to four feet long.

GRAND CANYON RATTLESNAKE *(Crotalus viridis abyssus)* This is the only rattlesnake endemic to the Grand Canyon. It is rare and found only on slopes and benches within the Canyon, not on the rim. These snakes bear live young. They are dirty-amber-colored with brown markings and a triangular head and can grow as long as three feet.

CHAPTER 9
Minimum-impact Travel

There's no doubt that with 600 people plus livestock living in a small area like Havasu Canyon, preserving and protecting the environment can be difficult. Add 30,000 tourists and the logistical aspects of waste removal to that equation, and you have a monumental environmental challenge.

Hiking in the Grand Canyon requires some special measures to maintain the desert's fragile ecosystem. In arid climates the difference between life and death is more tenuous, with scorching heat and scant rainfall. By minimizing your impact, you can do your part to keep the desert healthy and vibrant.

CAIRNS

Cairns, or small stacks of rocks, are placed on backcountry trails in some parts of the Grand Canyon to indicate the location of the trail. They can be particularly helpful on the slickrock surfaces of the Esplanade or in other areas where signage is nonexistent and the route is unclear. The use of cairns should be limited in accordance with Leave No Trace practices.

Most trails within Havasupai are well-established routes marked by a sign or defined by the course of the creek. Cairns can be found on some of the mesa trails in Havasupai and occasionally below Beaver Falls en route to the Colorado River, within the boundaries of Grand Canyon National Park. These cairns are generally appropriate and should not be moved or augmented.

CRYPTOBIOTIC SOIL CRUST

Cryptobiotic soil, also known as crypto-gamic or microbiotic soil, is a type of biological soil crust found throughout arid regions of the Grand Canyon and in much of the southwest. Cryptobiotic soil crusts are formed by living organisms and their

A cairn to mark the trail

byproducts, creating knobby clumps of soil particles bound together by organic materials. In parts of the Southwest, cryptobiotic soil crusts may represent 70 to 80 percent of the living ground cover. These organic crusts form nurseries for other plant forms trying to begin life in the desert.

Although these soils thrive on the undisturbed desert surface, they are delicate and can be quickly destroyed when trampled by the human foot. When you step on cryp-tobiotic soils, the dry and brittle fibers holding them together break down, become detached from the ground, and are subject to wind and water erosion. Once broken, the thin veneer of organic crust may take 10 to 50 years to regenerate.

Desert grass growing in cryptobiotic soil

Within Havasupai, cryptobiotic soils are most frequently found on the mesa trails and in the upper sections of Hualapai Canyon. To protect these nutrient-rich soils that nourish and foster the growth of other desert plants, take extra precaution to avoid stepping on them. In areas where cryptobiotic soils exist, stay on established trails. If you need to leave the trail, make an effort to walk on rock surfaces or in areas where you don't see an organic surface.

WASTE

For most of the 20th century, the Havasupai tribe disposed of waste at an open dump in Supai. There, the waste was burned to reduce volume, resulting in air pollution. Working in collaboration with the U.S. Environmental Protection Agency (EPA) over a nine-year period, the Havasupai tribe developed a new plan to remove waste and to protect Supai and much of Havasu Canyon. Implemented in 2006, the plan uses the existing tribal mule and horse packing enterprises to haul trash out of the canyon. The plan results in the proper management of approximately 196 tons of waste each year.

The environmental well-being of Havasu Canyon depends on all visitors being responsible for packing out their trash. Here are a few suggestions that will help you be a conscientious Havasupai visitor:

- Start by bringing in only those items you plan on using. Make sure they're packed in a way that can be easily compacted and taken out. Cans and many hard-plastic containers are difficult to crush and pack out with you. Bring a trash bag or other plastic bag to contain all of your accumulated trash while in camp, then pack it out.

- Remember that even waste such as food scraps and fruit peels can attract unwanted pests and take years to break down. If you bring it in, pack it out.

- Never leave food in the campground—either opened or sealed—as a "gift" to the next camper. If you bring it in, you must take it out.

- Resist the temptation to dispose of your trash in any of the trash bins in the village. The trash containers in the café and in the store are for local customers using those facilities and should not be used as a place to empty trash from your backpack.

- Never put your trash into one of the solar-assisted composting toilets.

- Before you leave, police your campsite for any food wrappers and small waste items such as glass, plastic, or metal. Even if it's not yours, pick it up and pack it out as a courtesy to the next camper.

CHAPTER 10
STAYING HEALTHY
IN THE CANYON

The Grand Canyon dishes out some extreme conditions that hikers from most other parts of the world are simply not used to. The sweltering heat and exposure to the desert sun demand extra precautions, planning, and preparation. Add to that the scrapes, lacerations, and other injuries that occur when playing around the waterfalls, pools, and creek, and you'll understand why a first-aid kit always gets a good workout in Havasupai.

On the hiking trails of Grand Canyon National Park, which adjoins Havasupai, park rangers assist about 500 debilitated hikers annually, most of whom entered the canyon unprepared for the heat, sun exposure, and physical demands of hiking in the desert. The ascent from Supai Village to Hilltop can be particularly brutal in midday sunlight. Even spring and fall temperatures can hover around 100°F.

Protecting a Hiker's Most Valuable Assets

Hiking into a canyon is the opposite of hiking up a mountain. You do the steep downhill first—which has both advantages and disadvantages. On the plus side, you can go quite a bit faster and it's not as exhausting. But the downhill trek can be demanding on both your feet and knees. A few precautions can save you significant discomfort.

FEET Wear sturdy, well-fitting boots with a sole that can protect you from the bruising of uneven trail surfaces. Your feet will sweat from exertion and heat, so wear absorbent hiking socks and have a dry pair to change into later.

KNEES Sturdy, well-fitting boots with a cushioning sole can absorb some of the shock on the downhill. Your best friend may be a pair of trekking poles. You are most likely to injure your knees as the muscles get tired, so take more frequent breaks if you feel any weakness.

HEAT-RELATED ILLNESS AND DEHYDRATION

Both heat exhaustion and the more serious heatstroke are very real risks in Havasupai, especially on trails that get significant sun exposure, such as the ascent to Hualapai Hilltop and the exposed portions of the hike to Beaver Falls and on to the Colorado River. Heat exhaustion occurs when body fluids are lost while exercising in hot weather, causing your body temperature to rise. Symptoms may include profuse sweating, thirst, weakness, dizziness, cramps, headaches or nausea, and a body temperature higher than 100°F. Untreated, these symptoms can lead to heatstroke, which is recognized by unconsciousness or an impaired mental state (confusion, hallucinations), hot or dry skin, elevated blood pressure, hyperventilating, and a core body temperature in excess of 105°F.

To combat these risks, during the warmest months of the year be sure to carry a liter of water with you and to drink and refill at every opportunity. Because you can sweat a liter of water per hour walking in the heat, there is also a risk of hyponatremia from drinking too much water and depleting the body's stores of electrolytes. To minimize this risk, maintain your caloric intake, particularly with salty foods like crackers, pretzels, and peanuts.

To treat symptoms of heat exhaustion, find a cool, shaded area where you can rest. Consume cool liquids such as water or electrolyte replacement drinks, apply cool water to the skin, or wade or sit in the cooling water of Havasu Creek. Loosen and remove clothing if necessary and do not consume any beverages containing alcohol or caffeine. If symptoms persist, or if any symptoms of heatstroke are present, get immediate medical attention.

SUNBURN

A bad case of sunburn isn't likely to result in death or a trip to the hospital, but it can certainly ruin a trip. Additionally, sunburn can permanently damage your skin and increase your risk for skin cancer.

Protect yourself by wearing a good sunscreen. If you are fair-skinned, choose 30 SPF or higher; otherwise 15 SPF should suffice. Remember to reapply every two hours.

Experienced canyon hikers generally wear a wide-brimmed hat that provides protection to the face, neck, scalp, and ears. Many also wear clothing such as a long-sleeved shirt and long pants. They find that loose-fitting comfortable clothing that covers most of the body not only provides sun protection but feels cooler in the direct sunlight.

BLISTERS

Blisters are common on the Havasupai Trail. Even if you're wearing a well-worn pair of shoes that have never given you blisters previously, you may find that the heat, the extended distance, and the added weight of a backpack can lead to an altered gait, plus additional friction that can result in blisters.

If you are prone to blisters—which are generally more common on the downhill portion of the trails—protect your feet with moleskin. Moleskin should be a part of any hiker's first-aid kit, and it's best applied before you begin hiking or as soon as you feel a hot spot.

Once a small blister has formed, you can cover it with an adhesive bandage. When you thus eliminate further rubbing and irritation, the blister often heals quickly and without further discomfort. As long as the skin remains unbroken, you have a natural barrier against infection. Don't puncture the blister unless it's large and painful enough to impede walking. To drain the fluid, sterilize a needle or sharp knife blade and make one or more small incisions near the edge of the blister. Drain the fluid and leave the overlying skin in place. Apply antibiotic ointment and cover with a bandage.

The entrance to the Mooney descent

CHAPTER 11
NATURAL HAZARDS

Flash Floods

It's a paradox that the most defining elements of life in a desert canyon are lack of water and too much water. The challenge of traveling in a parched environment and the potential for flash flooding are frequent concerns when exploring the Grand Canyon. Since 1898, Havasupai has experienced 17 major floods.

Torrential rains that have been known to dump 3 to 4 inches in a matter of a few hours can quickly fill dry canyons with a wall of rushing water capable of carrying large rocks, trees, livestock, and humans in its flow. Most of these flash floods occur during the monsoon season, from mid-July through August. As warm storm systems from the Gulf of California carry moist fronts toward the Colorado Plateau, they cool and unleash their water, often in violent and very localized patterns.

In August 1997 flooding led to the evacuation of Supai Village. During the flooding, electricity, water, sewer, and telephone service all went down. But with a quick response from the tribe and helicopter evacuation of more than 300 people, there was no loss of life.

The only flash-flood fatalities in recent history occurred in August 2001, as two adults and a young child hiking toward the village were caught in Hualapai Canyon floodwaters. One witness said the victims were caught in a 20-foot-high wall of water that "sounded like a 747 jetliner." The victims' bodies were recovered 3.5 miles up Hualapai Canyon from the village.

During monsoon season, heed flash-flood warnings. Do not enter Hualapai Canyon during a warning. In the campground, know where the high-ground campsites are located, and observe all advisories given by tribal authorities if you're asked to move to a higher campsite.

Over the Edge

Although it may seem a bit morbid at first glance, *Over the Edge: Death in Grand Canyon* is a landmark book and a fascinating read for any Grand Canyon visitor. In it, authors Michael Ghiglieri, a river guide, and Thomas Myers, a physician, chronicle every recorded death in the Grand Canyon with the aim of preventing future fatalities.

What they find is that very few people have died in the Grand Canyon, due to "bad luck" or an "unforeseeable incident." Instead, fatalities within the canyon result from a series of decisions that often begin with disregard for posted warnings and common sense. "Acts of God" rank low on the list as a cause for canyon fatalities; bad judgment ranks at the top. Readers are reminded that "there are no new accidents—only new people having the same old accidents."

The book also points to a "911 mentality" on the part of many visitors, who often make the misguided assumption that help will always be immediately forthcoming if they place themselves in harm's way. This sort of misguided thinking all too often proves lethal.

The Flood of August 2008

Even though seasonal flooding is a regular occurrence in Havasupai, no one expected the destructive deluge that tore through the canyon in August 2008. It was late summer, the monsoon season, when a light rain began falling in Supai. No one was particularly concerned. Suddenly, word came that upstream a downpour was sending a torrent of water that could be devastating and potentially deadly. Over 200 tourists were airlifted from the usually calm campground along Havasu Creek and given an unexpected helicopter ride to the canyon rim. Thankfully, prompt action eliminated any serious injuries or deaths—but the destruction to the canyon was inevitable.

On the afternoons of August 15, 16, and 17, 2008, thunderstorms dropped heavy rain over an area between the city of Williams and the Grand Canyon, producing significant flooding on Cataract Creek and the Havasupai Reservation. Total rainfall was generally light in the Supai area, but up to six inches fell within the Cataract Creek drainage southeast of Supai. This rainfall, along with the breaching of the Redlands Dam at the head of Cataract Creek, increased the flow of Havasu Creek from a normal 66 cubic feet per second to nearly 6,000 cubic feet per second. The typically crystal clear water of Havasu Creek turned to a sickening chocolate milk color as suspended rocks and gravel scoured a dramatic new channel. In a matter of hours, the face of Havasupai was changed forever.

Although Supai Village was spared significant damage, the narrow sections of the canyon that host the well-known waterfalls and quiet campground were ravaged by the raging floodwaters that flowed nonstop for nearly three days. Bridges were washed out, trees were toppled, and 1,600 feet of trails were obliterated or damaged. Navajo Falls, a favorite water playground of hikers, was suddenly sucked dry; in its place a plunging red canyon and three new waterfalls emerged. The fragile travertine aprons at the top of Havasu Falls were chipped and eroded, causing the falls to drop at a different angle into the aqua pools below.

The next destination for the floodwaters was the campground, where the gentle slope slowed the flow and caused the sediment and debris to drop, dumping approximately 450,000 cubic yards of silt and debris in the campground—and raising the elevation of the campground by six feet. Of the 90 picnic tables in the campground, only 3 escaped being buried under the sediment. Farther downstream, Mooney Falls and Beaver Falls had the least visible damage, but close examination reveals even these were battered by the immensity of the flood.

Recent canyon floods in 1990, 1993, and 1997 were still fresh in the memory of Havasupai tribe members. Destruction of trails, campsites, and bridges demand massive manpower to manage recovery efforts. In addition to the natural destruction, most tribal income, which depends heavily on campground revenue and packing, ceased with the flood. Following the flood, Havasupai was closed to tourists for over eight months while the campground, trails, and bridges were restored.

The Havasupai people, the "guardians of the canyon," recognize the natural events that inevitably cause changes to their desert home and were ready to repair the damage. With simple tools they took on the massive task of felling dead trees, removing debris, and sculpting the terrain so visitors could be welcomed once again into the "land of blue-green waters."

How to Avoid a Mountain Lion Attack

Mountain lions are generally solitary and elusive, and the potential for being attacked by one is extremely rare. Most mountain lions in Havasupai are found at higher elevations. Still, visitors to the backcountry should be prepared with knowledge that will help minimize the chance of an attack.

- **Do not hike alone.** Travel with groups of at least two or three.

- **Keep children close to you.** Mountain lions are more likely to attack a small child than an adult.

- **Do not approach a lion.** Never corner a lion; make sure that it has a way out.

- **Do not run from a lion.** Running will trigger a lion's instinct to chase. Instead, stand and face the animal. Pick up or hold on to small children.

- **Appear large.** Do not crouch or bend over. That will make you look like the lion's typical four-legged prey. Instead, raise your arms, make loud noises or wave your trekking poles. Let the lion know that you are not easy pickings.

- **Fight back if attacked.** Remain standing and facing the animal. Throw rocks and use sticks, tools, packs, or water bottles to fend off the attack.

INSECTS AND SNAKES

Biting insects are rare within the canyon, even in the summer months. Bats come out early in the dusk hours and seem to do a commendable job of keeping the insect population in check. Although mosquito bites are rare in the campground, you might want to bring a small container of insect repellent just in case. Along the trail, biting horse flies can occasionally be a nuisance.

Within the Grand Canyon are several species of rattlesnakes, several species of deadly scorpions, black widow and brown recluse spiders, killer bees, Gila monsters, hantavirus, and other venomous or noxious critters, none of which has ever caused a recorded fatality among the 5 million or so people who visit the Grand Canyon each year.

TRAIL HAZARDS AND FALLING

The trails within Havasupai are generally wide and well maintained. Tribal trail crews are constantly working to keep well-trodden trails in good repair. Trails located near precipitous drop-offs are often fenced off and are almost always marked by signs.

The descent down the cliffs to Mooney Falls is often seen as one of the more adventurous and hazardous areas in the canyon. While the climb down will certainly pose some challenges for claustrophobic, acrophobic, and inexperienced hikers, the chains and ladders protecting the route are secure. In fact, the route has an excellent safety record.

While there has never been a recorded fatality for someone making the descent through the approved tunnels and chain-and-ladder system, there was one incident in 2001 involving a visitor who attempted an off-trail descent of the cliffs by Mooney Falls. The teenage male, reportedly under the influence of amphetamines, initially edged himself to the lip of Mooney Falls with the intent of diving off, before bystanders talked him out of diving. He then tried to down-climb from the trail, without the protection of the chains, and fell about 100 feet to his death.

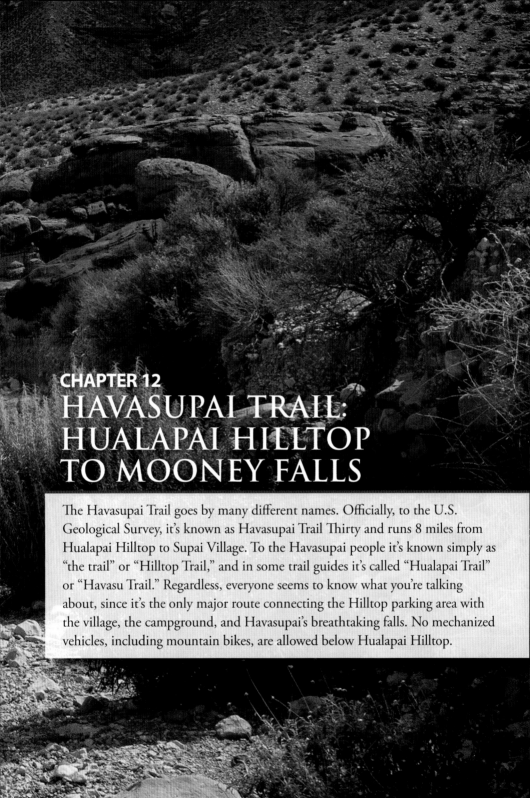

CHAPTER 12
HAVASUPAI TRAIL: HUALAPAI HILLTOP TO MOONEY FALLS

The Havasupai Trail goes by many different names. Officially, to the U.S. Geological Survey, it's known as Havasupai Trail Thirty and runs 8 miles from Hualapai Hilltop to Supai Village. To the Havasupai people it's known simply as "the trail" or "Hilltop Trail," and in some trail guides it's called "Hualapai Trail" or "Havasu Trail." Regardless, everyone seems to know what you're talking about, since it's the only major route connecting the Hilltop parking area with the village, the campground, and Havasupai's breathtaking falls. No mechanized vehicles, including mountain bikes, are allowed below Hualapai Hilltop.

HAVASUPAI TRAIL

General Description: The main trail connecting the Hualapai Hilltop parking area with Supai Village, the campground, and major waterfalls. The only maintained trail within the Havasupai Reservation.

Difficulty: Moderately strenuous

Trailhead location:
Hualapai Hilltop   N36° 09' 36" W112° 42' 34"

Trailhead Elevation and Total Distance: 5,196 feet, 11 miles one-way

Key Points:
1.3 Hualapai Canyon floor   N36° 10' 03" W112° 43' 14"

6.7 Junction with Cataract Canyon   N36° 13' 09" W112° 41' 29"

7.2 First bridge crossing of Havasu Creek

8.0 Supai Village center   N36° 14' 12" W112° 41' 20"

9.0 Uqualla Springs, Fiftyfoot Falls overview   N36° 14' 57" W112° 41' 48"

10.0 Havasu Falls viewpoint   N36° 15' 18" W112° 41' 55"

10.1 Campground (ranger office)   N36° 15' 24" W112° 42' 04"

11.0 Mooney Falls (base)   N36° 15' 46" W112° 42' 27"

Elevation gain/descent:
1,034 Hualapai Hilltop to Hualapai Canyon floor

893 Hualapai Canyon floor to Cataract Canyon junction

77 Cataract Canyon junction to Supai Village

352 Supai Village to campground

350 Campground to Mooney Falls (base)

Total descent, Hualapai Hilltop to Mooney Falls: 2,706 feet

Time Required:
Hualapai Hilltop to Supai: 2.5–5 hours

Supai to campground: 45–90 minutes

Campground to Mooney Falls (base): 15–30 minutes

(Times could vary widely based on physical condition, pack weight, weather, and breaks.)

Maps:
USGS *Supai and Havasu Falls*

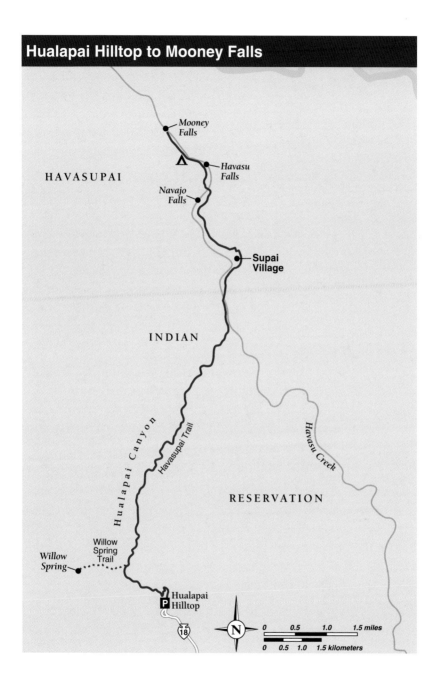

HAVASUPAI

Mooney
Falls

Havasu
Falls

Navajo
Falls

Supai
Village

INDIAN

Hualapai Canyon

Havasupai Trail

Havasu Creek

RESERVATION

Willow
Spring
Trail

Willow
Spring

Hualapai
Hilltop

18

N

| 0 | 0.5 | 1.0 | 1.5 miles |

| 0 | 0.5 | 1.0 | 1.5 kilometers |

The Havasupai Trail descends quickly into Hualapai Canyon and follows the dry canyon floor for 5.4 miles before merging with Cataract Canyon on the right to form Havasu Canyon. There are some large steps on the trail, but no climbing is required. The trail is largely exposed to sun, so plan your trip to avoid the midday heat.

The trail is well constructed, well used, and well maintained. The constant use by packers with their horse and mule trains, along with the cycle of rains and occasional flash floods, puts heavy demands on the trail. Trail crews from the village are constantly combating erosion and working to make the trail safe and serviceable to its thousands of users. While it's unlikely you'll get lost, some points along the canyon bottom require that you pay close attention in order to stay on the trail.

The solar-assisted composting toilets at the Hilltop parking area are the only toilet facilities for the next 8 miles until you reach the café, which has public restrooms with flush toilets. If the café is closed when you arrive in Supai, the next public toilets can be found at the campground, 2.1 miles down the trail, just north of the packing area.

There is no water available at the Hilltop parking area. The small RV that sells drinks is only open during daytime hours, and even then irregularly. Since most hikers leave early in the morning, always bring several gallon jugs of water in your vehicle. Make sure that each hiker in your party begins the hike well hydrated and with at least two liters of water in his or her pack. After leaving Hilltop, your next available drinking water will be at the Supai Tourist Office faucet, 8 miles down the trail.

Since the Havasupai Trail is shared by hikers and horses, remember that hikers must give horses the right of way.

HUALAPAI HILLTOP TO SUPAI VILLAGE

The Havasupai Trail starts at the far north side of the parking lot next to the packhorse staging area. The trail immediately dips below the rim before switching back to carve a giant sweeping loop into the western wall of the canyon's Coconino sandstone.

This section of trail is protected with some concrete reinforcements and steps. Along the way you'll be treated to some expansive canyon views before the trail emerges onto a broad, exposed ridge where the route flattens out somewhat.

Halfway to the canyon floor, Coconino sandstone gives way to talus slopes of Hermit shale and Supai sandstone, with desert vegetation of sagebrush and yucca. Along this ridge the trail widens and braids its way down the slope. Staying generally to the right tends to provide the best and most direct route to the canyon floor. At the base of the 1.3-mile descent, follow the canyon floor to your right.

Hualapai Canyon is a broad canyon and at this point measures more than a mile wide from rim to rim. As the route moves down-canyon, the trail descends, the walls rise, and Hualapai Canyon becomes a beautiful deep slot canyon for about 2 miles before merging with Cataract Canyon.

The First European on the Havasupai Trail

Led by Hualapai guides, Father Francisco Garcés descended the Havasupai Trail in 1776 and became the first European to visit the canyon. Garcés was a Spanish missionary based at the mission San Xavier del Bac, near present-day Tucson. He made extensive explorations of the Southwest both as a chaplain on the expeditions of Juan Bautista de Anza and on his own. His 1776 expedition was undertaken in search of a route from Sonora to Alta California.

At the time, no mules could use the trail, and some of the upper portions could be climbed only by using the ladders placed by the Indians. Upon entering the canyon, Garcés found 34 families of the "Yabipai Jabesua" tribe, whom he described as happy and hardworking.

Garcés spent many peaceful days with the Havasupai but never returned to the canyon. In 1779, Garcés was assigned to the San Pedro Mission on the Colorado River. Earlier, de Anza had promised the Yuma Indians that a larger mission would be built in the area. After three years of waiting, the Indians, feeling betrayed and angry, attacked the San Pedro Mission and killed Garcés and his fellow missionaries.

The trail is shared by horses and hikers from Hualapai Hilltop to the campground. Horses, either individually or as a pack train, can catch hikers by surprise, particularly as they come around a blind bend in the canyon at trotting speed. Horses have the right of way, so step aside and leave some clearance for both their pack and yours as you let them pass. Move to the side of the trail farthest from a cliff or exposed drop-off.

As you hike along the gravel base of the canyon, one strategy is to watch for more foot-friendly spur trails to the right or left of the main canyon wash. They are often shorter, better suited to foot traffic, and less likely to be used by horses. They often provide more scenic variety and are certainly less gravelly.

Weathered rock in Hualapai Canyon

After hiking about 2.7 miles along the wash, you'll come to a plastic sign on the right side of the wash indicating the 4-mile mark. This sign marks the halfway point between the Hilltop and the village. It's a good place to check your timing if you want to estimate your arrival time in the village or the campground.

As the canyon narrows, it cuts its way through the Esplanade sandstone and into the Supai formation, revealing deep rust-colored canyon walls. In this area you'll also come to the first perennial seeps of water, which appear as wet spots on the trail, or

View from Hilltop into Hualapai Canyon

sometimes just hoofprints filled with no more than a half inch of water. The most predominant spring comes into view about 0.2 mile from the Cataract Canyon junction. This perennial spring appears as small pools and trickles in sculpted terraces of mauve limestone, which play seasonal host to tadpoles. The trail crosses this spring and descends steeply to the right.

Soon the canyon widens and the mouth of Cataract Canyon emerges on the right. A sign in the center of the wash points left to Supai Village. You'll hear Havasu Creek to your right, and within about 0.5 mile a bridge will take you across Havasu Creek. From this point down to the bridges below Navajo Falls, the creek will be on your left (west) side, and largely out of view. Giant cottonwoods and willows provide ample shade.

After crossing the bridge you may want to hike on the berm that follows the irrigation canal to the right of the trail. This berm offers a hard, single-file surface and takes you away from the dusty horse path.

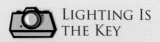

LIGHTING IS THE KEY

If all you want are some quick snapshots for friends and family, most any camera setup will do. However, if you hope to create landscape shots like those that grace the pages of *Arizona Highways,* consider the lighting demands of Havasupai. Avoid the harsh direct light and deep shadows of midday, as the broad contrast range simply overwhelms even the most sophisticated of cameras. When the sun goes behind the deep canyon walls or is lighting the walls above your prospective shot with magnificent "bounce light," you'll get even lighting that allows all the rich colors to emerge. If you're lucky enough to get overcast conditions, this creates even, rich lighting.

—*Derek von Briesen*

Coming over a small rise in the trail, the appearance of small houses and corrals signal your arrival in Supai Village. In just 0.5 mile you'll be in the village center, where you will likely be stopping at the Tourist Office on your left to register. From the Tourist Office you'll pass the helicopter landing area before arriving at the café on your left, where you'll probably want to take some refreshment before heading on to the campground and the falls. (Detailed information on the village can be found in Chapter 13, Supai Village, pages 83–89.)

SUPAI VILLAGE TO MOONEY FALLS

As you leave the village center, the trail, which is now the main street of Supai, jogs to the left around the gated schoolyard, then to the left again as you approach the Supai Bible Church directly in front of you. If you're looking for the lodge, you'll find it behind the church and to your right.

The trail leaves the commercial center of the village by crossing a gravelly wash followed by a right turn. With houses to your left and an irrigation canal to your right, the trail continues for 0.3 mile in the partial shade of cottonwood and mesquite.

After passing a small corral and the last house on your left, the trail rejoins the creek, and from this point down to Mooney Falls the creek will always be within view or earshot.

About 1 mile from the center of the village, the chasm below Fifty Foot Falls and Little Navajo Falls becomes visible on the left. You'll have good views of the new waterfalls created in 2008, when floodwaters carried away earth and rock and scoured the creek channel down to a hard rock layer.

In this area the trail is unstable, and plans are underway to reroute the trail to avoid the precipitous drop-off and to establish a more secure route should further flooding erode the trail completely.

In this area you'll notice a seepage called Uqualla Springs on the east side of the trail. It's a reliable but lesser-known source of pure drinking water, frequently used by tribal members.

Below the Fifty Foot Falls and Little Navajo Falls chasm, the trail previously crossed two footbridges, which were destroyed in the 2008 flood. As you cross the creek, now on your right-hand side, the canyon constricts and the creek's still water flow belies the exciting drop ahead at Havasu Falls. With a guardrail at your right, the trail makes a steep descent while offering an ideal vantage point for photos of Havasu Falls. At the end of the steep descent, you enter the horse-packing area, pass through a gate, and enter the campground. (Detailed information on the campground can be found in Chapter 14, Camping in the Canyon, pages 91–95.)

The trail continues for 0.6 mile through the campground, which stretches along both sides of the creek. At the north end of the campground the cottonwood grove gives way to

Signs at the junction of
Hualapai and Havasu Canyons

open sunlight and a cluster of solar-assisted composting toilets. Within 100 feet the trail quickly descends into travertine mounds and switchbacks approaching Mooney Falls. As you reach Mooney Falls, the canyon has cut its way through the Supai formation deep into the Redwall limestone, but the most notable geologic feature in the immediate area is the layers of chocolate travertine.

The adventurous climb through travertine tunnels and along a cliff protected by ladders and chains brings you to the base of Mooney Falls and the end of the Havasupai Trail. (Detailed information on Mooney Falls and the other falls and pools of Havasupai is found in Chapter 15, Waterfalls and Pools, pages 97–109.)

Moon over canyon rocks

CHAPTER 13
SUPAI VILLAGE

Supai Village has been home to the Havasupai Indians for many centuries. Today it has a population of about 600 people. Many of their homes line the trail as it winds through the village, while many more homes are located in the canyon to the west of the trail and out of view for most visitors. Most of the homes have large lots for farming and corrals for horses.

Supai Village

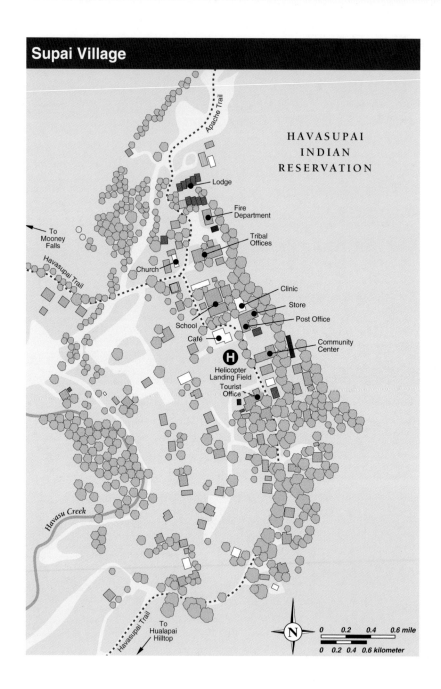

HAVASUPAI
INDIAN
RESERVATION

Apache Trail

Lodge

Fire
Department

To
Mooney
Falls

Tribal
Offices

Havasupai Trail

Church

Clinic

Store

School

Post Office

Café

Community
Center

Helicopter
Landing Field

Tourist
Office

Havasu Creek

To
Hualapai
Hilltop

Havasupai Trail

N

0   0.2   0.4   0.6 mile

0   0.2 0.4 0.6 kilometer

Supai is anything but a hot nightspot. The village shuts down as soon as the sun sets, and with no streetlights, people tend to stay inside their homes. Almost no porch lights or yard lights stay on to provide direction at night. If your plans take you into the village for the afternoon, be sure to bring along a headlamp to guide you back to the campground in the evening.

TOURIST OFFICE

This is usually the first stop for anyone staying at the campground. The staff will check you into the campground, issue your permit, make return horse arrangements, and help with instructions, directions, and a map. You can fill your water bottles at the faucet on the east side of the building. A retail area sells shirts, hats, books, and some local crafts and accepts cash, credit cards, and debit cards.

Hours: May–October, 6 a.m.–6 p.m.; November–April, 8 a.m.–5 p.m. (After-hours check-in is available at the campground ranger office next to the packing-station gate.)

CAFÉ

After the Tourist Office, the café is a good second stop, with ice-cold lemonade to refresh weary canyon hikers. It serves breakfast, lunch, and dinner and is best known for its Supai tacos and hot fry bread. The freshly baked cookies and nut breads make hearty trail snacks. The café accepts cash, credit cards, and debit cards.

Hours: May–September, 7 a.m.–7 p.m.; October–April, 8 a.m.–5:30 p.m.

GENERAL STORE

The general store carries basic food items, fresh meats, fruits and vegetables, and lots of cold beverages. Visitors can pick up food for cooking in the campground along with propane, ice, and postcards. The steps of the store seem to be a meeting place for villager and visitor alike. The store accepts cash, credit cards, and debit cards.

Hours: May–September, 6 a.m.–7 p.m.; October–April, 8 a.m.–5:30 p.m.

The Café in Supai

LODGE

The lodge is located behind the school and to the east of Supai Bible Church. Accommodations in each room include two queen beds, private bath, and air-conditioning. No telephone, TV, or roll-away beds are available. Free public Wi-Fi is available at the lodge and throughout the village center. All 24 rooms are nonsmoking.

Hours: 8 a.m.–5 p.m.

Reservations: Call 928-448-2111 or 928-448-2201.

U.S. POST OFFICE

All residents of Supai, Arizona (ZIP code 86435), receive their mail at one of the post office boxes. Visitors can buy stamps and mail cards and letters, each bearing a special mule-train postmark. (See the sidebar on page 88.)

Supai's Drinking Water

While camping in Havasupai, you will probably drink most of your water from Fern Spring. But where do the residents of Supai get their water?

The Havasupai—"people of the blue-green water"—view water sources as sacred, and they take water quality seriously. This is one of the few tribes in the United States to develop its own water-quality standard, one more rigorous than Arizona's state standard.

The drinking water in Supai is not taken directly from the creek but from a well field adjacent to the creek at a depth of between 78 and 150 feet. The water is treated at the well and pumped to the two water tanks above the village. These tanks deliver water with a steady and reliable pressure to homes throughout the village.

The water is naturally high in calcium and magnesium and has a slightly sweeter taste than what you may be used to at home. As you leave the village, fill your containers at the Tourist Office tap and take home some of Supai's finest beverage.

SUPAI MEDICAL CLINIC

Located to the left of the store, the medical clinic is operated for tribal members by the Indian Health Service, a branch of the U.S. Department of Heath and Human Services, and is staffed by a physician from the U.S. Public Health Service. The clinic has a small pharmacy and provides emergency medical treatment to visitors on a fee basis. The most common type of emergency treatment required is for heat exhaustion, followed by injuries resulting from climbing and jumping at the falls. More serious injuries or emergency surgical procedures may require air ambulance evacuation, which can cost you an easy $8,000—a strong incentive to use good judgment to remain safe.

SINYELLA STORE

Located on the west side of the trail, 0.5 mile south of the village center, this small store is your first opportunity to buy cold drinks on your way in, and your last chance to stock up on the way out. They stock white gas, propane canisters, and some camping supplies.

Hours: 7 a.m.–8 p.m.

Supai
Bible Church

Mail, Meals, and Mule Trains

If you think it's tough awaiting a long-expected letter, just imagine waiting for your dinner to arrive by mail. The residents of Supai, Arizona, ZIP code 86435, depend on the U.S. Postal Service to bring almost every item the town uses, including all their food. As a result, residents eat more mail than they read. When the only café in town runs out of a main ingredient, meal service grinds to a halt until the next mail delivery.

So how does mail get delivered to such a remote canyon? Unlike anywhere else in the United States, the postal fleet, established in 1896, is furry and four-footed—mules. Residents rely on these sturdy pack animals to deliver milk, meat, magazines, machines, and medicine. Much of what the village needs has a postage stamp attached. Sure-footed and carefully packed, the well-trained mules make the 8-mile trek each way with a payload of up to 200 pounds apiece. Fueled by grain rather than gasoline, the mules deliver almost 20 tons of mail a week.

Even though it takes several hours for mail to go up or down the trail by mule train, the cost is the same as if mailed from a typical post office. If you want to lighten your load on the way out, consider mailing your backpack home as you're leaving the canyon. And you can be sure that your hand-cancelled postcard from Supai will be a conversation piece when it arrives back home.

Teachers and schoolchildren

SUPAI BIBLE CHURCH

The distinctive chapel with its stone face and steeple has been a Supai landmark since 1948, when a helicopter brought in the military-surplus Quonset hut by "sling-load." Visitors are welcome to attend Sunday services at 9:30 a.m. and 11 a.m.

THE CHURCH OF JESUS CHRIST OF LATTER-DAY SAINTS

Mormons have had a longstanding presence in Havasu Canyon, dating back to Jacob Hamblin's visit in 1863, followed by frontiersman John D. Lee, who lived with the Havasupai for two years and introduced peaches and alfalfa to Native American farmers. The present white chapel, built in 2005, is located on the east side of the trail, 0.5 mile south of the village center. Sunday services begin at 11 a.m. and are open to visitors.

SUPAI MUSEUM

The museum is housed in the old stone building attached to the Tourist Office. It maintains a small collection of local historic artifacts, photos, baskets, and woven cradleboards. Admission is available on request through the Tourist Office.

CHAPTER 14
CAMPING IN THE CANYON

The Havasupai Campground stretches for more than a half mile along the banks of Havasu Creek below Havasu Falls. It once was the site of an old mining camp, and the mine shacks were still in place until the late 1940s. The present campground was constructed by the National Park Service in the 1960s to replace the shadeless site across from Navajo Falls.

The campground has tables and sites to comfortably accommodate 250 guests; but that number can swell to over 300 on peak spring and summer weekends. Considered "primitive" or "rustic," the campground is cradled in lush vegetation and crawling vines under the canopy of towering cottonwood trees.

ARRIVING AT THE CAMPGROUND

If you've already checked in at the Tourist Office, you can go directly to a campsite. Wheeled carts are generally available near the Ranger Station to carry mule-packed bags to your campsite. If you're arriving after the Tourist Office has closed, the camp check-in area is normally open to receive latecomers.

A day ranger is available 8 a.m.–5 p.m. for assistance. Night security is available at the Ranger Station during the tourist season from 7 p.m. to 5 a.m.

SHARING PHOTO-OPS

Havasupai is an exceptionally photogenic place, and you can always find other photographers at many of the key viewpoints. Be considerate of your fellow visitors and photographers. Because of Havasupai's renown as an iconic landscape photo opportunity, there will be times when many photographers are vying for the same shot. Be respectful and share, so all can enjoy and get what they came for. No one has priority over others. The Havasupai culture is strong in its belief in sharing, and this is a great opportunity to put that belief into practice.

—*Derek von Briesen*

SELECTING A CAMPSITE

Except for the large commercial group site at the upper end of the campground, specific sites cannot be reserved and are available on a first-come, first-served basis. Sites are not numbered or marked but can usually be identified by a table and tent area.

Nearly all campsites are within 100 feet of the creek, and many are right on the creek. Most campsites are well shaded by cottonwoods. Throughout the campground the creek is primarily flatwater, running two to three feet in depth with occasional pool drops of just one to three feet. Some of the campsites at the lower end of the campground are ideally situated near a particularly beautiful set of small (two- to three-foot) falls and pools.

If you have any difficulty finding a campsite, you might consider crossing the creek on one of the large timber bridges. The campsites on the east side of the creek are often the last to be claimed and are more secluded and quieter.

Some sites are designated as higher-ground areas where you can find safety during a flood. When flood waters threaten, rangers will instruct campers to evacuate to these higher sites.

WATER

The only source of drinking water for the campground is Fern Spring, at the upper end of the campground along the western wall. This spring produces about four gallons per minute from two white plastic pipes tapped into the canyon wall. The water is reliable and requires no treatment, but if you have any doubts, there is a small

metal tap on the north side of the brick building that delivers water from the spring that has been treated and chlorinated. Make sure you take your water directly from one of the pipes rather than from the trough below. Fern Spring should not be used for washing clothes or dishes.

The water from Fern Spring is actually water from Havasu Creek that has reentered the ground in a natural recharge zone just above Havasu Falls. Within days it reappears at Fern Spring as pure potable water.

Playing in the water of Havasu Creek as it flows through the campground is permissible, and it's especially enjoyable in the heat of the summer. The water is clean and safe for recreational use. Showers are not available in the campground, but you may bathe in the creek with biodegradable soap.

FOOD AND COOKING

While it's not necessary to hang and protect your food items as you would in bear country, be aware that camp robbers—stray dogs, as well as the more traditional squirrels, chipmunks, birds, and mice—are common around the campground and will get into food left out in the open. It's best to keep your food items securely closed in an airtight bag inside your pack or a cooler, then zipped up within your tent.

Some campsites have poles from which you can hang your packs and bags of food. Rangers patrol the campground and check for trash cleanup.

Campfires are not permitted in the campground. All cooking must be done on a backpacking stove or propane campstove.

LOOKING UPWARD

Don't forget to look into the sky. During monsoon season, the skies often have magnificent cloud formations that make for spectacular photos. The brilliant blue sky can be a great contrast against the deep-red layers. But don't include too much sky—just enough to frame the wonder of the canyon spread out before you.

—*Derek von Briesen*

Eat like a King in Havasupai

Wilderness camping demands a specific skill set when it comes to preparing meals. Freeze-dried food can be expensive and is often less than thrilling. Ramen can get pretty repetitive. Even trail mix loses its charm after a day or two. Monotony is the enemy. But weight and refrigeration requirements keep the most interesting foods off the menu. That is, unless you know the secret to gourmet backpacking.

The horses that bring the mail down to Supai Village can also be hired to bring in a camp stove, full ice chest, and a well-stocked pantry of fresh foods. The horses can haul an entire kitchen down the trail for you at a reasonable cost if it is properly packed and evenly distributed. If you have a large group, this is a great way to go. Open fires are not permitted in camp, but with a propane-fueled grill and griddle, imagine the meal that could greet you after a long day of hiking: grilled steaks or salmon, cool green salad, fresh fruit and vegetables, lemonade, and pastries or chocolate mousse for dessert. Plan an Asian night with your favorite stir-fry recipes, or a Mexican dinner with fajitas from the grill. It's all possible if you plan carefully. Since you'll be packing out any waste, you'll find that an empty cooler lined with a trash bag is a convenient and efficient way to pack out your trash.

WASTE MANAGEMENT

The solar-assisted composting toilets in the campground are similar to those used at the campgrounds in Grand Canyon National Park. Composting toilets have largely replaced the Porta Potties previously used in the campground. Since composting toilets have capacity limitations, Porta Potties may still be in use during peak spring and summer season to meet peak demand.

Never put inorganic items, trash, or food waste in the composting toilet. The Leave No Trace principle of "pack it in—pack it out" is especially important in Havasupai. Do not think you can bury or burn trash, or dispose of it in toilets. You are responsible for packing out your garbage and food scraps.

Solar Composting Toilet

The solar-assisted composting toilets available to the public in Havasupai are among the most technologically advanced, environmentally friendly outdoor waste systems in use today. They recycle human waste by converting solids and liquids into compost. Oxygen is drawn through wood shavings so that bacteria can break down organic matter without an unpleasant odor.

To keep these toilets in proper working order, use only toilet paper. Do not put inorganic items, trash, or food waste into the composting toilet. Close the lid after use. Never put anti-bacterial wipes into the toilet, as they do not decompose and actually inhibit the composting process. The composting toilets have a capacity of 100–120 uses per day per stall.

BACKCOUNTRY CAMPING

Camping below Mooney Falls or in any other area of the Havasupai Reservation requires advance Tribal Council permission.

If you plan on hiking down to the Colorado River into Grand Canyon National Park, be aware that there is no camping within 100 yards upstream and 0.5 mile downstream of Havasu Creek's confluence with the Colorado River. No camping is allowed between Beaver Falls and the Colorado River. Be sure to let rangers or others in your party know if you plan to hike down to Beaver Falls or beyond.

WORKING WITH YOUR CAMERA: LENSES

Here's a quick note on lens selection. This will be key to the creation of a variety of stunning photos. A good wide-angle lens is important to capture all the beauty of the major falls. A telephoto at the long end of your zoom range will also yield good results with some of the smaller, more distant falls as well as more distant sites as you hike canyon trails. The telephoto will also allow you to capture some of the many gorgeous close-up subjects that adorn the walls and creek bank.

—*Derek von Briesen*

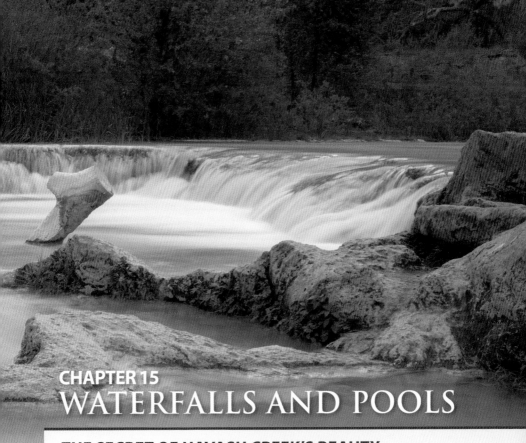

CHAPTER 15
WATERFALLS AND POOLS

THE SECRET OF HAVASU CREEK'S BEAUTY

The first question everyone asks at the first glimpse of the pools at Havasu Falls is: "What makes the water so brilliantly blue?" The short answer is—minerals.

It's not the minerals in the water. Rather it's the minerals that have precipitated out of the water. The entire base of the pools is covered in a smooth, creamy-white travertine that reflects the color of the blue sky overhead through the crystal-clear water. When the sun is high, the shallow pools around Havasu Falls become a brilliant shade of aqua.

PHOTOGRAPH-ING THE FALLS

Because the major falls are so huge, it's often difficult to get them without some sort of significant shadowing. This is where getting up early or staying late will pay rich dividends. Also, cooler temperatures in the morning and evening hours reduce the number of people you may be disturbing at the falls. Find a place below the small cascades in the creek and shoot upstream.

—*Derek von Briesen*

The process that created this spectacular and unique environment has taken centuries and continues to evolve. The water in Havasu Creek has traveled underground for nearly 100 miles through layers of limestone, sandstone, shale, and more limestone. These layers hold water-soluble minerals, easily absorbed with the presence of carbonic acid in the water. When the water reaches the surface, just upstream from the village, it is saturated with minerals held in suspension.

Once above ground, these carbonates precipitate, meaning they separate from solution or suspension. When this happens, the carbonates create the features that give Havasu Canyon its unforgettable personality.

Creamy base of the pools Some carbonates fall as light-colored deposits that cover the bottom of the creek and pools. Each pool and creek bed may seem slightly different in color as the travertine base reflects a blend of the tones from surrounding green vegetation, brown cliffs, and blue sky.

Natural dams Some of the carbonates adhere to rocks, logs, and other organic matter in the stream. This buildup leads to the formation of natural dams found in the canyon near the base of the falls, creating pools, small drops, and water diversions. Note the travertine buildup on the chains at Mooney Falls or on the tree roots at Havasu Falls as indicative of how fast this process takes place.

Caves and grottoes Flanking each of the falls you will find various inlets into the formation. Some are large enough to enter, others just worth peering into. They are created by both deposition of carbonates and erosion from fast-moving or percolating water. These fascinating features are fun to explore.

Aprons, skirts, and veils These exceptional features are created by mineral-laden mist from waterfalls settling on the surrounding canyon walls and rocks. As the water in the spray evaporates, the minerals are left behind. When the carbonate-bearing mist combines with airborne fine red sand, rust-colored aprons, skirts, and veils are draped around each of the falls.

Starting in the village area, several small natural dams begin to form, but you'll notice that there are very few pools above Havasu Falls. This is because Havasu Falls aerates the water and accelerates precipitation. The aeration and precipitation intensifies around the falls, which explains the spectacular natural dams, pools, and travertine formations immediately below Havasu, Mooney, and Beaver Falls (and Navajo Falls until its destruction in the flood of August 2008). Beyond Beaver Falls the gradient of the creek decreases, the carbonate content of the water is reduced, and very few natural dams exist.

All of the major falls are located in the Redwall limestone strata of the canyon. Limestone is more resistant to erosion than the overlying Supai sandstone layer. Redwall limestone also erodes in benches, creating precipitous drops. Grand Canyon hikers know that these Redwall cliffs and benches provide some of the most memorable sections of trail in the canyon. In Havasu Canyon, these same cliffs produce the Grand Canyon's most spectacular waterfalls.

The splendor of Havasupai's falls and travertine pools is exclusive to Havasu Canyon —a spectacular oasis in a stretch of parched desert wilderness. Nowhere else in the world will you find the abundance, accessibility, and stunning beauty of the falls and pools of Havasupai.

ENJOYING THE FALLS AND THE POOLS

Havasu Creek flows from its source at a fairly consistent rate throughout the year. Except for flooding brought on by heavy rains, the creek depth will rarely vary more than a few inches. Similarly, water temperature in the creek normally remains between 66 and 72°F. This is pretty chilly for most swimmers, but refreshing for play on a hot summer day.

Havasu Creek near Beaver Falls

Under normal conditions, playing in the pools below the falls is generally safe and enjoyable, although subject to the risks inherent in any outdoor physical activity or water sport. But under flood conditions, all bets are off.

Floods can happen throughout the year, although they are most likely to occur in the monsoon season during July and August. Dark storm clouds and a visible rainstorm in the distance could signal an impending flash flood, even if it's not raining where you are. If you find yourself caught in a rainstorm or if you hear floodwaters approaching, you should leave the area below the falls and get to higher ground. Rangers stationed in the campground and at Havasu Falls will often alert visitors to imminently hazardous conditions and advise evacuation of flood-prone areas.

The travertine rims that create the smooth lips on the pools are solid and not slippery as they appear. They generally make a safe crossing point if you walk on top of or just behind the rim. While the water going over the rim is often just an inch or two deep, you may find a deeper channel on either side of the rim, where the depth quickly drops to two or three feet and the current becomes powerful and treacherous for crossing.

Don't try playing around these falls barefooted. River sandals or aqua socks offer protection and better traction. After you've checked the depth of a pool, jumping in feet first can be fun. Be aware that after heavy rains, water can be murky, making jumping more dangerous.

The depth of the water below the falls and the uneven surface on the bottom of the pools make diving especially hazardous. Climbing on the travertine faces behind the falls and diving from rocks or ledges around the falls are prohibited by the Havasupai tribe. Take care approaching all of the falls, as the soil is unstable and the drop-offs are often unprotected.

Fifty Foot Falls
(photo courtesy of
iStock©fremme)

FIFTY FOOT FALLS

Location: Viewed from Havasupai Trail, starting about 1 mile north of the village
N36° 14' 47" W112° 42' 01"

Elevation at base: 3,100 feet

Height: 75 feet

Time: Located 30 minutes from the campground; allow 2–4 hours for your visit to Fifty Foot Falls and Little Navajo Falls

Access: Easily accessible from the main trail

Immediately following the flood of August 2008, in which the new waterfalls were created, this waterfall—the largest of the new waterfalls—was given the temporary name New Navajo Falls. But within a couple of years it was officially named Fifty Foot Falls. In a canyon that's constantly changing, there is no such thing as a permanent name. Fifty Foot Falls is near the area where the old Fiftyfoot Falls once flowed. Prior to 1900, George Wharton James made visits to Havasu Canyon in which he referred to it as Havasupai Falls. Others have referred to falls in this area as Hualapai Falls. These historical references may all refer to the area once known as Fiftyfoot Falls, which at the time may have been about 50 feet high.

But the flood of 2008 scoured the channel; removed much of the silty soil, along with considerable earth, rock, and vegetation; and lowered the creek bed to a bedrock base. As a result, the Fifty Foot Falls you see today has emerged as a higher version of the old Fiftyfoot Falls and in a different location than its predecessor.

LITTLE NAVAJO FALLS

Location: Viewed from Havasupai Trail, starting about 1 mile north of the village
N36° 14' 50" W112° 41' 54"

Elevation at base: 3,065 feet

Height: 30 feet

Time: Located 30 minutes from the campground; allow 2–4 hours for your visit to Little Navajo Falls and Fifty Foot Falls

Access: Easily accessible from the main trail

This waterfall was created during the flood of August 2008 and was given the temporary name of Rock Falls, but is now officially known as Little Navajo Falls (although some signage refers to it as Lil Navajo Falls). This waterfall is closer to the trail and more accessible than Fifty Foot Falls and has a nice swimming hole at its base.

Little Navajo Falls with Fifty Foot Falls in the background (photo courtesy of iStock©zysman)

HAVASU FALLS

Location: Trailhead on Havasupai Trail   N36° 15' 21" W112° 41' 56"

Elevation at base: 2,923 feet

Height: 95 feet

Time: Located 10 minutes from the campground; allow 2–3 hours for your visit to Havasu Falls

Access: From the south (upper) end of the campground, go up the Havasupai Trail 0.1 mile to a cluster of scattered trails to your left. A walk of about 200 feet leads you through a short prickly-pear obstacle course and over a travertine rise to the base of the falls.

Havasu Falls is the most popular and most photographed of the Havasupai falls. As with many of the major falls, the appearance of Havasu Falls has changed over time. Before 1954, the creek fell in two divided streams into the pool below. A massive outcropping of travertine jutted out from the center of the falls about halfway down the wall, breaking the water's freefall.

Today you're more likely to see what appears to be a single-column direct plunge. You will be awestruck by its beauty, power, and extraordinary lushness in such a harsh desert.

Following the flood of 2008, the top of Havasu Falls is about five feet lower, and the water shoots out to the side, making it less dramatic and less symmetrical than before the flood. However, more of the travertine aprons have been exposed.

Today Havasu Falls is easily accessed from the Havasupai Trail. Most visitors make it their first stop, since it's only a 10-minute walk from the campground. Havasu Falls is also a popular spot for wedding ceremonies and renewal of vows. If you want to make special arrangements for this type of use, contact the Tourist Office in advance.

Most visitors to Havasu Falls spend an hour or more at the base of the falls, relaxing on the broad beach in the shade of giant cottonwoods or playing in the downstream pools. To the right of the falls is a grotto shrouded in watercress. Inside are some unusual travertine formations, although any stalactites that may have once been present have been destroyed. Near the base of the cave is a small perennial spring that flows into the pool below Havasu Falls.

PHOTOGRAPHING HAVASU FALLS

The classic shot of Havasu Falls from the side of the trail is almost always a late-afternoon shot, with the sun well behind the canyon walls. Early afternoon produces a pronounced shadow line at the pool below Havasu Falls, which you'll probably want to avoid. Havasu Falls can be photographed from high above the valley floor on West Mesa Trail (see Chapter 16, pages 128–130), a hike best undertaken in spring or fall.

—*Derek von Briesen*

One of the best places to position yourself for a day at Havasu Falls is on the grassy area on the left (east) side of the main pool. You'll have good morning shade and a perfect view of the falls without being in their constant spray. To get there requires that you cross the rim. But once there, you'll find it to be quieter and more secluded than the dirt area immediately in front of the falls. This site also puts you at the mouth of Carbonate Canyon, where you can explore the canyon and mine on a short hike. (For more information about Carbonate Canyon, see the hike description in Chapter 16 on pages 119–120.)

Havasu Falls from the West Mesa Trail

Stay later until Mooney Falls is lit only by reflected sky or light bouncing off the walls above and you'll have a magical image. Many places along the steep switchbacking trail provide wonderful perspectives. The falls can be photographed from high above the valley floor on West Mesa Trail (see Chapter 16, pages 128–130), a hike best undertaken in spring or fall.

—*Derek von Briesen*

Flooding in Havasu Canyon

Havasu Creek is the second largest tributary of the Colorado River in the Grand Canyon. While perennial stream flow seldom exceeds two cubic meters per second, large floods can swell the creek in both winter and summer. Summer floods typically occur during the monsoons of July and August, while winter floods are the result of an unusually large snowfall immediately followed by a warming and sudden melt. More than 80 percent of Havasu's major floods have occurred during or immediately following El Niño years.

Prior to 2008, the largest flood on record occurred on January 2, 1910, followed by major summer floods in 1935 and 1954. A large flood occurred in September 1990 following several days of intense thunderstorms, when the creek flow peaked at more than 20,000 cubic feet per second. The flood caused severe damage to Supai, killed hundreds of ash trees, and altered many of the travertine pools and deposits near the falls.

Havasu Falls pool

MOONEY FALLS

Location: N36° 15' 46" W112° 42' 27"

Elevation at base: 2,490 feet

Height: 195 feet

Time: Located 15 minutes from the campground; allow 1–3 hours for your visit to Mooney Falls

Access: For many visitors to Havasupai, the most exciting part of Mooney Falls is just getting to the falls through the tunnels and down the chains and ladders fixed into the cliff. As you leave the campground, the trail descends through travertine outcroppings until Mooney Falls comes into full view. The trail leads directly to a tunnel, about 25 feet long, carved into the travertine cliff, followed by a second tunnel, about 15 feet long. Emerging from the second tunnel, a system of firmly planted stanchions, chains, and ladders guide your nearly vertical 120-foot descent down crudely cut steps in the travertine cliff. Take extra precaution during inclement weather or when the rock is wet. Small children will need assistance negotiating some of the larger steps.

With a plunge of 195 feet, Mooney Falls has a greater drop than Niagara Falls and is the highest in Havasupai. It is also regarded by the tribe as the most sacred of the falls. Mooney Falls is set in a deep enclosed canyon, which gives it an intimate and secluded feel. The cliffs surrounding the falls are covered with travertine skirts while maidenhair fern dots the base. The challenging route to the base of the falls, which goes through tunnels and down a cliff, may weed out the claustrophobic and acrophobic.

At the base of Mooney Falls is an oval pool with a deep-blue hue, the largest of all the pools in Havasupai. This main pool quickly fans out to a broad, shallow wading and walking area. Immediately below the wading area are several small pools with drops of two to five feet, ideal for playing and climbing.

One frequently asked question is whether the caves used to access Mooney Falls are natural

Mooney Falls ladder, circa 1905

or man-made. While the placement of these tunnels originally began around a natural opening, the square corners, carved steps and uniform height and width indicate that any natural opening was later enlarged by blasting and chiseling. Natural grottoes and passageways can be found at Beaver, Havasu, and Mooney falls. As you stand at Mooney Falls, note the large veils of travertine that adorn the falls on both sides and the dozens of pockets and passageways that exist behind those veils. The tunnels we use today were likely carved and enlarged from a smaller passageway in the travertine.

The Death of Mooney

The story of Mooney, a sailor-turned-prospector who fell to his death at the falls now bearing his name, is shrouded in mystery and lore. The miner was referred to as James Mooney in one early account, but the 1879 mining claim for Havasu Canyon identifies the prospector as D. W. Mooney.

As Mooney attempted the first descent of the cliff by means of a rope lowered from the top, the spinning rope caused him to lose his hold just a few feet from the rim and fall to the rocks below.

Alphonso Humphreys, one of the miners who shared the claim with Mooney, detailed Mooney's death in a letter:

"I well remember the trip that Mooney fell. We had been down in the canyon about three days when Mooney fell and was killed, and we had no way to get down and bury his remains.

"The next morning before any of us was up, Doheny went down to the cliff to see if Mooney had moved. He untied the rope and tossed it down with Mooney's boots and said 'This is all the funeral I can give you this time.'"

The next year the miners returned and found a Havasupai man who showed them a small cave leading to an overhang along the bank. They made the cave larger and blasted out a slanting tunnel, made the steps, and suspended one of their party on a rope.

The miners buried Mooney's limestone-encrusted body on a small island below the falls. By 1900 nothing remained of Mooney's grave.

BEAVER FALLS

Location: Beaver Falls descent on Havasu Creek Trail   N36° 16' 56" W112° 43' 46"

Elevation at base: 2,350 feet

Height: 50 feet

Time: Located 3 miles and 1.5–2 hours from the campground; allow 4–6 hours for your trip to Beaver Falls

Access: (See Chapter 16, Havasu Creek Trail: Mooney Falls to Beaver Falls, pages 112–115.) From the Havasu Creek Trail, on the narrow east mesa above the creek, watch for a trail that makes a steep descent to the creek. If you come to a view of Beaver Canyon on your left (the west side of Havasu Creek) and the sign announcing the boundary with Grand Canyon National Park, you've gone too far. Turn around, backtrack about 150 feet, and look for the steep slope descending toward the falls through the Temple Butte limestone cliffs leading down to the creek.

Beaver Falls, because of its remote location 3 miles downstream from Mooney Falls, is the least-visited of Havasupai's falls. But don't let the distance scare you off—Beaver Falls is an exceptionally photogenic setting that is worth the hike.

The falls cascade over a multilayered array of terraces and pools dotted with fern and watercress. They also provide the perfect playground for climbing and discovering the various pools.

Less than 10 percent of visitors to Havasupai make it to Beaver Falls, so your photos will give you some bragging rights. Beaver Falls can be easily included as part of a longer trip to the Colorado River or a hike up Beaver Canyon, just a few minutes downstream.

Beaver Falls

NAVAJO FALLS (DRY SINCE THE 2008 FLOOD)

Location: Trailhead on Havasupai Trail   N36° 15' 04" W112° 41' 54"

Elevation at base: 3,045 feet

Former Height: 90 feet

Prior to the flood of 2008, Navajo Falls was regarded by many as the most beautiful of all the Havasupai waterfalls. It scattered water across a 150-foot-wide shield of travertine nearly 100 feet high. Sheets of water cascaded down dozens of travertine aprons into an intricate system of pools with long, unbroken rims. The main pool at the base of Navajo Falls, now filled with mud, was once a broad, deep pool, ideal for swimming and diving. The grottoes of Navajo Falls were especially inviting.

Throughout the past 100 years, the appearance of Navajo Falls has changed frequently and dramatically. At various times it has been broad and lacy, as it appeared immediately prior to the 2008 flood, or narrow and gushing. While it's impossible to predict the course of the creek over time, it is difficult to imagine that the creek will ever shift back to the west and restore water flow to Navajo Falls.

Chief Navajo

Navajo Falls, which was destroyed in the flood of August 2008, was not named directly after the neighboring Navajo tribe but after a 19th-century Havasupai leader, Chief Navajo. As chief he negotiated the first treaty with the U.S. government in 1882. Navajo was chief of the Havasupai for 40 years before his death in 1898.

Navajo Falls after the flood of 2008

Navajo Falls before the flood of 2008

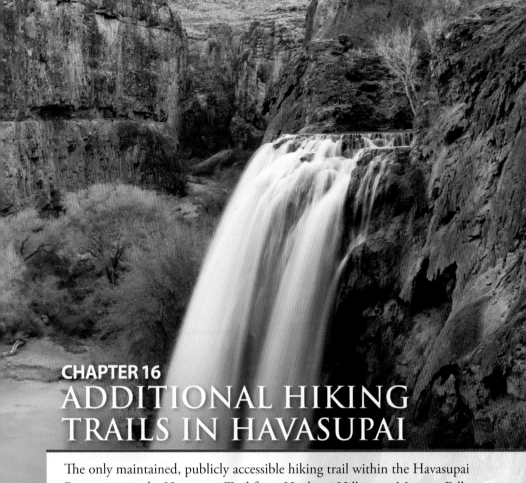

CHAPTER 16
ADDITIONAL HIKING
TRAILS IN HAVASUPAI

The only maintained, publicly accessible hiking trail within the Havasupai Reservation is the Havasupai Trail from Hualapai Hilltop to Mooney Falls. All other trails are considered unmaintained, backcountry, or wilderness trails. These unmarked trails see infrequent use; some of them can go days, weeks, or even months without visitors. Cairns are rare in Havasupai, and there are no signs identifying the trailheads. These trails can be overgrown with vegetation and difficult to follow. When hiking one of these paths, it's common to lose the trail, miss creek crossings, and have to backtrack.

Your best bet is to refer to the distance and difficulty rating for each trail and select those suited to your experience level. Never hike alone, and come prepared with navigational tools (map, compass, and/or GPS unit) in addition to other hiking essentials. Let others in your party know where you are going and when you expect to return.

HAVASU CREEK TRAIL: MOONEY FALLS TO BEAVER FALLS

General description: A day hike to Havasupai's most distant falls

Why go: To discover the exceptional beauty of Havasu Creek below Mooney Falls and to see Havasupai's most remote waterfall

Trailhead location: Base of Mooney Falls N36° 15' 46" W112 ° 42' 27"

Distance: Located 3 miles and 1.5–2 hours from the campground; allow 4–6 hours for your trip to Beaver Falls

Difficulty: 5 miles round-trip

Elevation gain/descent: 140 feet

Time: 3–4 hours

Tips and precautions: Partially shaded. Get an early start to avoid peak summer sun. Hike requires 3 easy creek crossings.

From the base of Mooney Falls the trail hugs the west canyon wall and ascends to a west ledge above the creek. At 0.1 mile you'll see the mouth of Ghost Canyon to your left. You may want to stop by for a quick visit now, or come back later for a more relaxing experience.

About 200 feet downstream from the mouth of Ghost Canyon, be sure to look for the old iron ladder fixed into the canyon wall to your left. At the top of this 150-foot ladder is the large opening of the old Cataract mine.

The first creek crossing takes place about 0.1 mile below the mouth of Ghost Canyon or about 0.2 mile below Mooney Falls. An easy ford, with water up to your calves, puts you on the east side of the creek. Another 0.1 mile brings you to your second shallow crossing, easily achieved over a broad travertine rim.

Fixed rope ascent on the trail to Beaver Falls

Mooney Falls to Colorado River

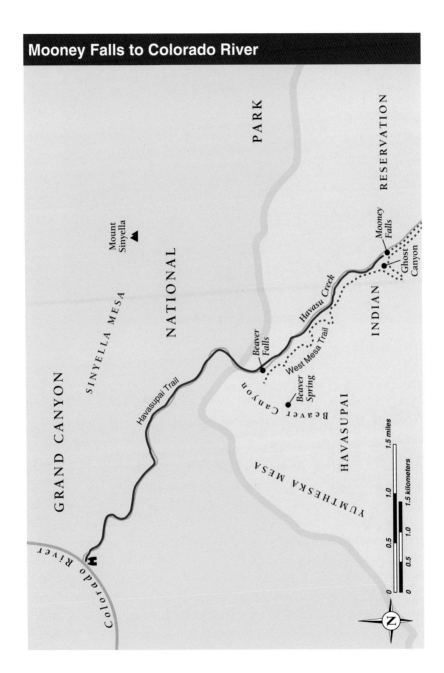

GRAND CANYON

SINYELLA MESA

NATIONAL

PARK

Mount Sinyella

RESERVATION

Mooney Falls

Ghost Canyon

INDIAN

Havasu Creek

Beaver Falls

West Mesa Trail

Havasupai Trail

Beaver Spring

Beaver Canyon

HAVASUPAI

YUMTHESKA MESA

Colorado River

0   0.5   1.0   1.5 miles

0   0.5   1.0   1.5 kilometers

N

Havasu Creek below Mooney Falls

Now on the west side of the creek, you enter a beautiful, broad, vine-covered plateau. The trail winds through this rise on the west side of the creek for nearly a mile. Through much of this area the creek will be out of sight, though rarely out of earshot.

As the plateau finally gives out and descends toward the creek, you'll make your third crossing. This time, water will reach up to your thighs, but not much higher than 24 inches. From this crossing the trail stays near the creek level until you come to a fixed rope–assisted climb up a 10-foot travertine cliff. The location of the rope climb is most easily identified by a large palm tree just 20 feet upstream on the creek's eastern bank. This may be the only palm tree you'll see in the Grand Canyon. Palm trees are considered a nonnative invasive species within Grand Canyon National Park and Havasupai. Since the 1970s, about a dozen palm trees have appeared in the Grand Canyon. It is not known whether their introduction is a result of avian or human intervention. Regardless, this landmark tree is flourishing.

Once you've climbed the cliff, the trail winds up and down through a desert ledge of cactus and mesquite. Looking down to your left, you'll notice that the creek is dropping more quickly in a series of small falls and rapids. After about 0.3 mile on this section of trail, watch for a steep descent to the creek down Temple Butte limestone cliffs. If you arrive at the National Park boundary sign on the trail, you've gone too far north. Backtrack about 150 feet and watch for the descent to the creek.

Once you're at the creek, a short upstream exploration puts you at Beaver Falls, while a crossing to the west leads you to the broad mouth of Beaver Canyon.

HAVASU CREEK TRAIL: BEAVER FALLS TO COLORADO RIVER

General description: A challenging day hike along Havasu Creek to the Colorado River

Why go: To claim bragging rights of a Grand Canyon rim-to-river hike, and for a best chance to spot a great blue heron

Trailhead location: On the trail above and to the north of Beaver Falls
N36° 16' 56" W112° 43' 46"

Distance: 8 miles round-trip from Beaver Falls or 15 miles round-trip from the campground to the Colorado River

Difficulty: Strenuous

Elevation gain/descent: 740 feet

Time: 4–6 hours (or 7–10 hours from campground)

Tips and precautions: If you're starting at the campground, get a predawn start in summer. There are many creek crossings, so if you decide to do the hike in river sandals, make sure they are also comfortable enough for hiking rugged desert terrain. Hiking poles will give you a real advantage on creek crossings.

In the Havasupai language, the Colorado River is known as the "big water." A hike from the campground to the big water of the Colorado is the ultimate Havasu Creek adventure. Even in the peak spring season the trail is rarely used and you may not see another person until you arrive at the river and meet up with rafters who will wonder how you got there.

This hike provides the best opportunity for sightings of great blue herons nesting in the riparian vegetation of Havasu Creek in spring and summer. The travertine-rimmed pools are rare below Beaver Falls, but the creek retains its clear beauty and offers many shady coves and ledges where you can relax or play in the pools.

A trip to the Colorado must be done as a day hike, since the national park does not issue overnight backcountry permits for Havasu Canyon and the tribe does not permit camping below Mooney Falls.

MID-STREAM PHOTOGRAPHY

If you're careful, setting up your tripod midstream often offers a "right there" perspective. If you get close, use a wide-angle; from farther away, a mild telephoto can produce an interesting perspective. Be sure to include the foliage and cliffs that surround the waterfalls, as the color contrasts will be dramatic and pleasing. The curves of the pour-offs often make great subjects just by themselves; shoot small sections close up and keep an eye out for reflections of foliage and cliffs in the flat water just above the pour-off. An eye for small details will be rewarded handsomely with unique and highly original captures.

—*Derek von Briesen*

Harvey Butchart Hikes to the Colorado River in 1946

If at any point between Mooney Falls and the Colorado River you complain about the trail being too rugged, consider what Harvey Butchart encountered when he first hiked the route in 1946.

Dr. John Harvey Butchart (1907–2002) is a Grand Canyon hiking legend. Harvey hiked more than 12,000 miles in the Grand Canyon, the most of any person in recorded history.

On his first visit to Havasupai he recorded that "the most impressive thing I did . . . was to walk to the river and back." At that time there was no trail from Mooney Falls to the river, where for long stretches the route was overgrown with a dense tangle of vines.

"Jean Rowe had told me about killing seven rattlesnakes on the way to the river, so I carried a big stick to defend myself. I wondered how I would ever see the rattlers under the tangle of growth. There were places where I tried going along the base of the cliff in order to pass the worst thickets. . . .

"Toward the river I got rather high on the slope to get away from the vines and I slipped and came down with one hand on sharp limestone and the other on a barrel cactus. It took a long day of struggle to go from our camp near Havasu Falls to the Colorado River and back."

After passing Beaver Falls you'll see the mouth of Beaver Canyon to your left. A metal sign on this desert rim marks the indefinite boundary of Grand Canyon National Park. The trail from Beaver Canyon to the Colorado River is actually easier to

Harvey Butchart

follow and more clearly defined than is the trail from Mooney Falls to Beaver Falls. You might be tempted to just call the creek your trail and start wading downstream, but if you stick with the trail, and watch for the cairned creek crossings, you should be able to make it safely to the Colorado with just five creek crossings. From the boundary down to the Colorado River, the ill-defined trail moves back and forth from creekside to desert ledge.

Once you pass the sign and enter Grand Canyon National Park, you'll make four creek crossings in near succession. After the fourth crossing, you'll spend about 90 minutes hiking on the east side of the creek. Nearing the river, the trail arrives at a beautiful area of red-rock patios, where you'll often find rafting parties enjoying a midday excursion and picnic in the shade of deep canyon walls and rock overhangs. Here you'll cross the creek to the west side and ascend the trail along some rocky ledges. As the creek narrows to a 20-foot slot canyon, the trail rises high above and soon arrives at the Colorado River.

This will require that you use some good judgment and occasionally scout the trail for the best crossing point.

The mouth of Havasu Creek is a popular stop on Colorado River trips.

Mining in Havasu Canyon

Mining has a long but ultimately unprofitable history in Havasu Canyon. From 1879 to 1901, the primary focus of mining was for lead and silver ore. During this period about 100 tons of high-grade ore was shipped to smelters. But since the canyon was 55 miles from the nearest railroad, high packing and mining costs made the operation a failure.

In 1902, the Grand Canyon Gold and Platinum Company was formed to prospect the lower region of Havasu Canyon for platinum near the Colorado River. The company spent about $75,000 attempting to build a road from Hilltop down into the canyon. The remains of this road are still used today where the Havasupai Trail descends into Hualapai Canyon. Neither gold nor platinum were found.

Havasu Canyon mining operations focused around five separate claims. The three most actively worked were the Bridal Veil Claim, encompassing the area around Havasu Falls and up into Carbonate Canyon; the Seligman Claim in the area of the present campground; and the Cataract Claim surrounding Mooney Falls. The Bridal Veil mine is still accessible near the mouth of Carbonate Canyon, and the Seligman mine is easily accessible on the west wall above the campground. The Cataract mine is inaccessible, but the remnant of an iron ladder on the cliff is still visible high on the west wall downstream from Mooney Falls.

During the period prior to World War I, there was a mining office, cabins, mill site, and a small smelting operation set up in the area where the campground now lies. The mines produced lead, vanadium (an additive for stainless steel, titanium, aluminum, and other alloys), zinc, small amounts of silver, and amethyst.

Mining came to an end in 1942, when a man named Sanderson purchased a lease on the Bridal Veil Claim in Carbonate Canyon. His operation extracted and shipped 164 tons of ore and had a return of only $8,500. More than half of the operation's expenses were consumed in packing the ore to the rim and hauling it to the nearest railroad terminal. Even under the wartime bonus prices for lead, the operation was a financial failure and the claim was foreclosed.

CARBONATE CANYON

General description: A dry side canyon tucked away behind Havasu Falls

Why go: To see Havasupai's best abandoned mine

Trailhead location: Base of Havasu Falls   N36° 15' 18" W112° 41' 51"

Distance: 1.5 miles round-trip

Difficulty: Easy

Elevation gain/descent: 150 feet

Time: 1–2 hours

Tips and precautions: Bring a headlamp if you want to explore the mine. The main tunnel of the mine is reasonably safe.

Carbonate Canyon is easily accessed beneath Havasu Falls by crossing the main rim over to a grassy area to the left of the falls. Climb through some of the brush on a small mound, and instantly the canyon awaits your exploration.

Carbonate Canyon is a flat-bottomed canyon about 200 feet wide at the mouth, within about 0.2 mile narrowing to about 50 feet. On the south wall, about 200 feet from the mouth, is an old mine shaft. By climbing the tailings to the opening you'll see some old mining equipment and ventilation holes to the right. These ventilation holes were used to pipe air into the deep lower chamber. The main shaft, where the metal mining cart rails are still in place, is relatively safe to explore, but don't enter alone or without an extra flashlight or headlamp.

Near the end of the main shaft, a side tunnel appears on the right. This side tunnel continues for about 80 feet and connects to a larger chamber to the left, marked by a low wood wall. The old ropes are unreliable, and the lower chamber has wood floors, which also pose a safety risk. If you do go into the mine, be sure to bring an extra headlamp.

Continue up the canyon for an additional 0.5 mile to a fork. The shorter finger to your left leads up a steep and narrow rocky ravine before it deadends into a steep 50-foot wall and becomes impassable.

The right finger continues up for 0.1 mile to a climbable but highly technical wall. The most interesting feature is a pool drop chasm carved through the graywall by water erosion. The large pool is filled with water year-round. Both fingers of the upper canyon are worth exploring.

Carbonate Canyon is an easy way to extend your stay at Havasu Falls and discover some of the canyon's rich mining history.

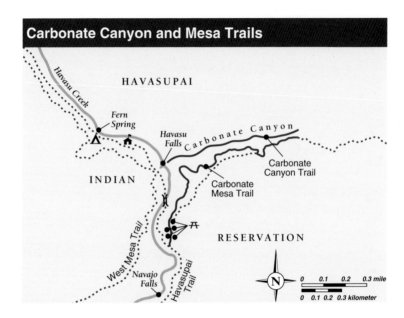

Carbonate Canyon and Mesa Trails

CARBONATE CANYON MESA TRAIL

General description: Short spur to an overlook of Havasu Falls and the campground

Why go: To see Havasu Falls from the top down

Trailhead location: On the Havasupai Trail above Havasu Falls
N36° 15' 01" W112° 41' 51"

Distance: 1.2 miles

Difficulty: Easy

Elevation gain/descent: 75 feet

Time: 30–45 minutes

Tips and precautions: No shade; most enjoyable in early spring and fall

About 100 feet up the Havasupai Trail from the old Navajo Falls overlook is a trail leading onto the broad mesa to the east via the Carbonate Canyon Mesa Trail. Along this gently rolling trail you'll pass several concrete tables that were used when this area was a campground. Mesquite, prickly pear, and agave cactus dot the mesa.

The trail leads to a precipitous viewpoint that gives you a bird's-eye glimpse of Havasu Falls, its pools, and down to the campground. The promontory puts you in position to see some sweeping views of the campground below Havasu Falls, the cemetery, and Carbonate Canyon to the north and east.

Count on an easy, reasonably flat out-and-back spur trail. There's no water or shade, so it is not recommended for a midsummer midday hike.

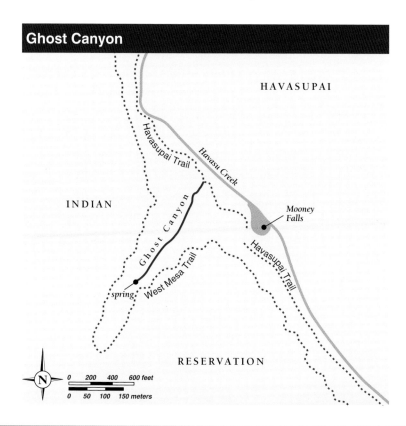

GHOST CANYON

General description: A deep and serene side canyon near Mooney Falls with a natural spring

Why go: To find shade, peace, and water within minutes of the campground

Trailhead location: Base of Mooney Falls   N36° 15' 46" W112° 42' 27"

Distance: 0.4 mile from the base of Mooney Falls

Difficulty: Easy

Elevation gain/descent: 100 feet

Time: 20–30 minutes

Tips and precautions: Easily accessed from Mooney Falls or on the way to Beaver Falls. A great place to escape the midday summer sun.

In earlier times, ashes of cremated Havasupai were placed here, leading to the name Crematory Canyon, and eventually Ghost Canyon. It enters Havasu Canyon from the west about 0.1 mile below Mooney Falls.

Ghost Canyon is a deep and narrow canyon, with steep sides 300 to 400 feet high. It's fed by a warm-water, fern-covered spring. At the top of the canyon are several large choke stones. You can scramble your way through the choke stones and see the terminus of the canyon, which receives some seasonal runoff, but the beauty of the canyon is found below these choke stones, where the springs emerge.

Ghost Canyon is a beautiful retreat where you can escape crowds and spend a few peaceful hours. You could spend the entire day in the cool shade and never see another person. The distant babbling of Havasu Creek and the falls is faintly audible.

Once you've hiked to the top of the canyon and made your return to Mooney Falls, walk about 150 feet downstream along the west bank of Havasu Creek to enjoy walking under the grotto of Ghost Canyon Springs as it cascades into Havasu Creek. One hydrological survey identified more than 50 springs on the Havasupai Reservation, of which Ghost Canyon is the most easily accessible.

Grotto below Mooney Falls

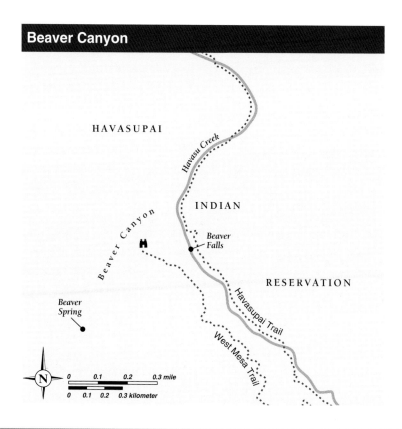

Beaver Canyon

Beaver Canyon

General description: A rocky side canyon, the largest along Havasu Creek

Why go: To experience the fun of navigating a canyon strewn with giant boulders

Trailhead location: On the trail above and to the north of Beaver Falls
N36° 16' 56" W112° 43' 46"

Distance: 1–5 miles round-trip from Havasu Creek, depending on how far up the canyon you want to explore

Difficulty: Strenuous

Elevation gain/descent: 200 feet

Time: 1–4 hours

Tips and precautions: Beaver Canyon provides one of the best opportunities for spotting desert bighorn sheep.

The mouth of Beaver Canyon is easily viewed to the west from the desert trail on the east side of Havasu Creek. To access Beaver Canyon, follow the Havasu Creek Trail into Grand Canyon National Park (a metal sign marks the boundary) and descend the limestone cliffs just downstream from the mouth of the canyon. You can also access Beaver Canyon from Beaver Falls, but the lower approach involves an easier creek crossing.

At its mouth, Beaver Canyon is dry. While earlier surveys have reported a perennial spring about 0.5 mile from the mouth, it now appears to be more of a seasonal occurrence. Still, there are numerous pools and basins to attract bighorn sheep and other animals year-round.

Just 100 feet from its mouth is a large choke stone the size of a small cabin that is easily skirted by climbing the cairn-marked cliffs on the north wall of the canyon starting about 50 feet below the boulders. Navigating several other large choke stones requires some scouting and probing, but it's all doable without a rope or technical climbing hardware.

Beaver Canyon might more appropriately be called "Rock Canyon" for its abundance and variety of rocks of all shapes and sizes. The canyon ascends slowly, nearly flat, for the first mile or so through red sandstone and giant limestone boulders. The vegetation is a mix of mesquite, willow, and cottonwood.

Beaver Canyon is a challenging day hike for those coming to Beaver Falls, and a great setting in which to study the rocks carried and eroded by the canyon's powerful floods.

Ladder at the confluence of Havasu Creek and Colorado River, circa 1900

George Wharton James's Adventure in Beaver Canyon

"For years, I have endeavored to reach the junction of Havasu Canyon with the main canyon of the Colorado River but have not yet succeeded," wrote explorer George Wharton James in 1899.

"Others starting from the village claim that they have stood where the pure blue waters of Havasu Creek mingle with the dirty red of the Colorado, but my efforts have not been crowned with success."

A Havasupai guide suggested James ride along the plateau above Mooney Falls (see West Mesa Trail) and descend through Beaver Canyon. With his guide, horses, and three days' provisions, James set off on the journey.

They soon arrived at a narrow spot in the canyon blocked by a large boulder. The guide suggested they turn around, but James suggested they drop a rope into the pool below and swim across.

"We undressed. I carelessly threw the rope over a boulder and asked him to fasten it." The guide jumped into the pool without tying off the rope. As James jumped into the pool, the loose rope followed him.

Now they were in trouble. They had no rope to climb back up to where their horses waited, and while they could hike up Havasu Creek, they would have to return to the village bare-foot and naked.

They ingeniously spent the afternoon building an underwater tower of rocks. With James standing on top of the pile, the guide climbed out of the pool and secured the rope for James's successful exit.

James never did make it to the Colorado.

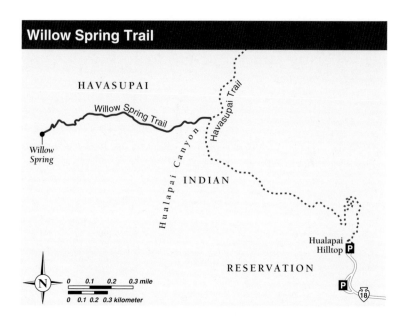

Willow Spring Trail

General description: A small side canyon with a natural spring

Why go: It's the closest water source to Hilltop

Trailhead location: Hualapai Canyon floor below Hualapai Hilltop
N36° 10' 03" W112° 43' 18"

Distance: 1 mile to spring, 2 miles to top of canyon, round-trip

Difficulty: Easy

Elevation gain/descent: 200 feet

Time: 30 minutes–1 hour

Tips and precautions: Willow Spring can be used as an emergency water source and shade spot in summer.

Willow Spring is located in the side canyon directly across the floor of Hualapai Canyon, where the trail descends from Hualapai Hilltop. Horses can often be found pasturing in the canyon and around the springs.

From the Hualapai Canyon floor, follow the dry wash up this side canyon. Although you won't find any willow in the canyon, after 0.4 mile you will begin to see moisture on the trail and the spring located just another 50 feet up the wash
(N36° 10' 04" W112° 43' 41").

Another 0.5 mile up the canyon won't take you near any more water but can offer shade under large rocks and steep canyon walls.

While it would be difficult to fill a water bottle at this spring, you could use a pump-type purifier to help suck water out of the small holes and pockets where it accumulates. The spring isn't much, but the horses sure know about it, and it could be a lifesaver if someone were suffering from severe dehydration and were absolutely unable to make the ascent to Hilltop. If you're going to use it as a water source, you'll find the purest flow 50 feet upstream from where the spring first appears.

Apache Trail

The Apache Trail is one of many trails used to access Havasu Canyon. It ascends near the water towers on the north side of the village but is no longer accessible to the public.

The Apache Trail derives its name from a raid in which Apache Indians used the trail to enter Havasu Canyon. Although no contemporary accounts of the raid exist, some historians believe the raiders were likely the neighboring Yavapai tribe, as it occurred prior to Geronimo's surrender in 1886. Some later versions of the story place Geronimo at the scene, but it was likely carried out by some of his band.

One account tells of the Apaches coming down the trail on foot early in the morning. The whole hillside, above where the water tanks sit today, was covered with 500 or 600 Apaches. With the Havasupai gathered in a fort, the Apaches crossed the creek and a skirmish ensued, both sides exchanging arrows.

The Havasupai brought in additional fighters from settlements downstream and were eventually able to fend off the Apaches, who returned back up the Apache Trail.

Every society has a boogeyman to deter bad behavior in the next generation. Even today, Havasupai parents will tell their unruly children to behave ". . . or the Apaches will come and take you away."

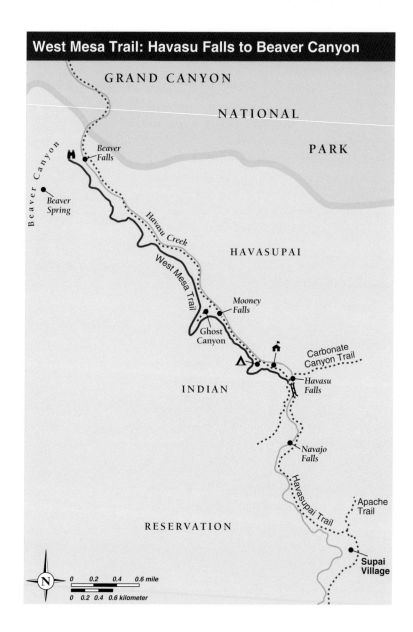

West Mesa Trail: Havasu Falls to Beaver Canyon

GRAND CANYON

NATIONAL

PARK

Beaver Canyon

Beaver Falls

Beaver Spring

Havasu Creek

West Mesa Trail

HAVASUPAI

Mooney Falls

Ghost Canyon

Carbonate Canyon Trail

Havasu Falls

INDIAN

Navajo Falls

Apache Trail

Havasupai Trail

RESERVATION

Supai Village

N

0   0.2   0.4   0.6 mile

0   0.2   0.4   0.6 kilometer

West Mesa Trail: Havasu Falls to Beaver Canyon

General description: A trail that parallels Havasu Creek along the Esplanade

Why go: It's the best "view trail" in Havasupai

Trailhead location: On the Havasupai Trail between Havasu Falls and old Navajo Falls   N36° 15' 15" W112° 41' 53"

Distance: 3.4 miles to second Mooney viewpoint, 8.8 miles to Beaver Canyon, round-trip

Difficulty: Moderately strenuous

Elevation gain/descent: 250 feet

Time: 1.5–2 hours to second Mooney overlook, 3–4 hours to Beaver Canyon

Tips and precautions: The trail has no water and is virtually shadeless for most of the day. It's best hiked in spring and fall.

To access the trail from the campground, take the Havasupai Trail passing Havasu Falls. From the top of the steps at Havasu Falls, continue 200 feet along the trail. To the right you'll see some faint trails through a mesquite thicket leading to a large fencepost at the cliff. By scrambling about 150 feet up the cliffside drainage, and following the cairns, you'll come to a well-defined trail on the mesa above. Turn left and follow this trail as it parallels Havasu Canyon on your right.

Beaver Falls

Once on the mesa the trail is well cairned and easy to follow. It is mildly undulating and only dips significantly as you skirt the head of Ghost Canyon just below the first Mooney Falls overlook. The first Mooney Falls viewpoint is impressive, but the second is arguably the best view in the entire canyon.

WATER, WATER EVERYWHERE

Plan ahead to keep your camera dry and your lens free of splashes. Many of the best photo angles demand that you stand in the middle of flowing water. The best advice for working in water: Always keep your camera's strap around your neck, even when the camera is mounted on the tripod. Tripods fall, especially in the sometimes unstable soft silt of the creek bottom; the neck strap will save your camera time and again. Keep a soft, absorbent towel handy to wipe off the spray, and don't drop your camera into the creek!

—*Derek von Briesen*

The large pile of rocks near the second Mooney viewpoint (N36° 15' 50" W112° 42' 41") was originally placed by early miners to mark the boundary of their claim. In this case, it's the northwest boundary of the Cataract Claim. The iron ladder and mine opening can be seen on the cliff as you hike below the pools at Mooney Falls.

You can continue hiking an additional 2.7 miles down to Beaver Point. If you go only as far as the second Mooney overlook, you've caught the best of the trail. Below Mooney Falls, the trail maintains the same basic elevation, although it does occasionally detour to the west to skirt some smaller side canyons.

In many ways, this is the most classic Grand Canyon hike in Havasupai. On the mesa you are surrounded by Arizona desert vegetation like ocotillo, cacti, and spring wildflowers. You'll see the scat of predators like coyote and mountain lions that populate the mesa, while desert bighorn find refuge on the higher cliffs. From the Beaver Falls overlook you'll have broad views of the Sinyella Mesa and Mount Sinyella to the east. Throughout the hike you'll be treated to the far-reaching upper canyon views only possible once you emerge from the depths of Havasu Canyon.

APPENDIX

GUIDES AND TOUR OPERATORS

Havasupai is a great do-it-yourself destination, but there are also many professional guides and tour operators whose years of experience can enhance your vacation immensely.

Arizona Outback Adventures
Offers multiday trips in Havasupai
aoa-adventures.com, info@aoa-adventures.com
866-455-1601 or 480-945-2881

Derek von Briesen
Leads guided photography expeditions in Havasupai
dvbphotography.com
928-821-2568

Discovery Treks
Small-group adventures with both camping and lodging
discoverytreks.com, adventures@discoverytreks.com
888-256-8731 or 480-247-9266

Just Roughin' It Adventure Company
Offers multiday trips in Havasupai
justroughinit.com
877-399-2477 or 480-857-2477

Pygmy Guides
Offers multiday trips in Havasupai
pygmyguides.com, pygmyguides@pygmyguides.com
877-279-4697 or 928-707-0215

Road Scholar
Educational adventure for active adults
roadscholar.org
800-454-5768

Southwest Outside Adventures
Specializes in custom and private groups
southwestoutside.com
928-284-1816 or 928-821-1929

Timberline Adventures
Includes Havasupai as part of Grand Canyon trips
timbertours.com
800-417-2453 or 303-664-8388

The Wildland Trekking Company
Offers small-group adventures in Havasupai
wildlandtrekking.com
800-715-4453

INDEX